UNIVERSITY
OF FLORIDA
LIBRARIES

PUBLIC ADMINISTRATION STUDY NUMBER 1

HANDBOOK

for

MASSACHUSETTS SELECTMEN

EDWIN A. GERE, JR.

and

ROBERT P. BOLAN

BUREAU OF GOVERNMENT RESEARCH

UNIVERSITY OF MASSACHUSETTS

AMHERST

The Bureau of Government Research is a research, training and service organization within the University of Massachusetts. It was established in January, 1956.

The functions of the Bureau are: (1) to conduct research in significant local and state governmental problems; (2) to provide research material in the social sciences for faculty and students; (3) to organize training institutes for public officials; (4) to furnish consultative services to governmental units; and (5) to serve as an information center for persons interested in public problems.

STAFF

William G. O'Hare, Jr., Director
Gerald J. Grady, Assistant Director
Edwin A. Gere, Jr., Assistant Director
Edward T. Dowling, Research Assistant
Hazel J. Tilton, Administrative Secretary
Kathleen M. Dansereau, Secretary

First Edition, 1956
Second Edition, 1960

Published by
Massachusetts Selectmen's Association
6 Beacon Street
Boston, Mass.

Price per copy $1.00

Mail all orders for copies to the Association.

Foreword

It has been often said that the difference between government by leadership and government by rulership is very real. Without delving deeply into the philosophical content of these contradictory terms it may be deduced that leadership is related to democracy while rulership implies monarchial, oligarchical, or totalitarian methods of government. In the United States, democracy is generally understood to mean the free choice by majority will between alternate candidates to serve as the officers of government and the subsequent dedication of these officers to the promotion of the general welfare while being mindful of the rights of all men.

The Massachusetts town from an early date served as the fertile field for the growth of the seeds of direct democracy through the development of the long ballot, general suffrage, and the open town meeting. Actually, the election of selectmen, or "selected men," dates from the middle of the seventeenth century, and to the present they have been looked upon as the coordinating leaders of their respective town governments. Changes have naturally been visited upon the towns with the passage of time so as to equip them with the proper legal and political means to respond to the challenges and popular needs of the modern moment; nevertheless, there are no two towns in the Commonwealth that are identical in all aspects of government—no more than there are any two towns with the self-same populations and problems.

Yet, in spite of this anomaly, there are many points of general accord, and it is to the identification of those that affect the office of selectman that this publication is dedicated. Its object is to bring together the many provisions of the laws that touch upon that particular office, in an orderly and understandable manner, so that each selectman may have a more thorough view of the duties and responsibilities that are generally attributed to a board of selectmen in Massachusetts. Every effort has been made to prevent omissions. Perusal should clearly delineate the need for a close and continuing cooperation between the board of selectmen and the town counsel if interpretive error is to be avoided and the rule of law advanced.

At this point it seems wise to indicate that the town is a most important entity of local government in Massachusetts—in fact, 312 of the 351 municipalities in the state are constituted as towns, and, by way of information, no town has been chartered as a city for four decades. Thus it is that the selectmen of the Commonwealth are both numerous and influential public officers who give generously of their time to the public service without substantial remuneration.

The Bureau of Government Research expresses its gratitude to the members of the Executive Committee of the Massachusetts Selectmen's Association and to its officers—John E. Finnegan, Vincent P. O'Brien, Richard J. Kent, Charles W. Knowlton, and Thomas J. Callahan—for their continuing interest in this revised edition of the handbook and for underwriting the publication costs. The enthusiasm of Fred C. Emerson, Raymond M. Trudel, and Charles W. Davis, past presidents of the state association, is also acknowledged.

Mrs. Hazel J. Tilton of the Bureau staff prepared the manuscript.

The original research was conducted by Robert P. Bolan, former Bureau staff member, now of Providence, Rhode Island.

WILLIAM G. O'HARE, JR.
Director

Amherst, Massachusetts
September, 1960

TABLE OF CONTENTS

	Page
FOREWORD	3
GENERAL ROLE OF SELECTMEN	7
GENERAL POWERS AND DUTIES	10
Alcoholic Beverages	10
Boundaries	11
Building Inspection	11
Civil Defense	12
Coastal Waters	12
Districts	14
Dogs	16
Elections	17
Finance	19
Fire Department	23
Fire Prevention	24
General Administration	25
Grade Crossings	27
Health	29
Highways	30
Housing and Redevelopment	34
Licenses	35
Low Lands and Swamps	38
Militia	39
Municipal Lighting	40
Nuisances	41
Planning and Conservation	42
Playgrounds and Recreation	43
Police	44
Public Works	45
Schools	46
Sewers	47
Town Meetings	47
Town Officers and Employees	49
Town Property	52
Vacancies in Office	53
Water Supply	54
Welfare	55
Zoning	56

TABLE OF CONTENTS—(*Continued*)

POWERS AND DUTIES OF SELECTMEN RELATIVE TO PUBLIC UTILITIES..	58
General	58
Electric Companies	58
Electric Railroads	59
Gas Companies	60
Railroads	60
Street Railways	61
Telephone Companies	64
Water Companies	66
REFERENCE TO GENERAL LAWS CONCERNING SELECTMEN	67

General Role of Selectmen

Nature of the Office

Perhaps nowhere in American government can there be found a public office as unique as that held by selectmen. Originated in Massachusetts and confined to New England, the office has enjoyed an unbroken tradition of respect and authority since Charlestown first used the term "selectmen" in 1634. All New England states except Rhode Island have continued and preserved to the present day this form of local government. As our young nation grew and its people began to push westward, they carried with them and put into practice in their new communities many of the principles of democratic rule for which they had been willing to wage a Revolutionary War. While the selectmen form of government itself has never become transplanted in other regions of our expanding country, the basic idea, or the principle of government by committee, has found its way at one time or another into thousands of communities across the land.

Although weighted by over 300 years of tradition and hampered by an overlapping of boards, commissions and functions, the selectmen form of government in Massachusetts has maintained its popularity in the face of such changes as rapidly increasing population, more complexities in governmental administration, and rising costs of goods and services. Its popularity without a doubt can be attributed to the fact that this form of government is adaptable to changing conditions. Its historic prestige may be maintained while its operational structure is streamlined to meet the demands of the twentieth century. In short, it is a workable form of government.

Responsibilities of Selectmen

For Massachusetts town government to function at highest efficiency requires a certain sense of responsibility on the part of selectmen. Once organized, the machinery of government may coast along on its own momentum—very often with little direction from town leaders. Reports may be made, bills may be paid, and business may continue as usual. However, in this kind of atmosphere other events will generally take place as problems mount up with little or no ameliorative action taken, lethargy sets in and indifference prevails. Selectmen have a responsibility to avoid such conditions in local government. It is their obligation to create the kind of community atmosphere and to provide the kind of leadership that looks beyond tomorrow, that looks beyond the borders of the town, and that works in the best interest of all the people. In this respect selectmen are more than merely administrators and signers of reports. They are at once legislators, executives, politicians, planners, informed citizens and a host of other personalities. They each wear a dozen hats. They work full-time at a so-called part-time job. They are out nearly every night attending various meetings. Their time belongs to the public, yet they love every minute of it.

In this kind of frenzied atmosphere how may selectmen's responsibilities best be channeled into action?

Answers to this question can only be in the category of opinion, yet it seems that because selectmen have so many responsibilities they are both physically and mentally immersed in their duties much of the time. But because they do engage in mentally rewarding work, they are in a most advantageous position to enhance the prestige of their office and their community. A few applied principles may be beneficial here.

Involved as they are in the endless activities of their position, selectmen have opportunity to foresee trouble, to take effective action and in so doing forestall a crisis. In other words there is a need for them to look ahead and to approach town affairs from the long range as well as the day by day point of view. In handling these along with everyday situations, they should recognize that effective public communication on their part will insure an accurate, rather than a rumored, relating of events.

It is a selectman's responsibility at all times to inform his fellow townsmen of both routine and significant events occurring in local government. Selectmen are so named because they were chosen to carry out the daily affairs of the town, with the implication that the people would remain informed. Their responsibility in this area should not be limited to an annual report.

Communication, of course, is a two-way street. Nothing can be of greater moral support to selectmen in a vital decision than the knowledge that it is based on the general will. Searching out and securing this "sense of the community" is another major responsibility if selectmen would be true to their office. A concerted effort to insure that a cross section of the community is represented on appointive boards and commissions will do much toward ascertaining the will of the people.

Selectmen have a further responsibility to recognize that Massachusetts town government, in all its flexibility, has practical limitations. As stated before, the structure of selectmen government may be altered to meet the demand of today while at the same time preserving its traditional prestige. But even flexibility has a breaking point. Here the selectmen must look abroad to find solutions to those problems not easily answered within the community. This type of responsibility is made up not so much of vision as of courage and extra devotion. Its rewards are found in the numerous fine examples of regional and intermunicipal cooperation evident in the Commonwealth today.

Finally, selectmen have a responsibility to gain a working knowledge of their general powers and duties as defined by law. This point, it might appear, should be too obvious to mention; nevertheless, it is no simple task to acquaint oneself with approximately 700 sections of law relating directly to selectmen and with hundreds of other sections bearing on town government in general. It is hoped that this handbook will serve selectmen in their quest for such a working knowledge.

Purpose of the Handbook

This study presents a digest of the more important laws and sections of law pertaining to the office of selectmen. Its purpose is to relate in nontechnical language short summaries of the law according to subject matter classification. This handbook should not be used as a substitute for the law but rather as a general guide. Selectmen, when acting in an official capacity on a specific subject, should refer to the exact wording of the statute. Quite frequently the laws contain certain exceptions and express various shades of meaning not easily described in narrative form.

To assist selectmen in using this handbook in conjunction with the statutes, a reference to the General Laws by chapter and section number is provided in the final section.

General Powers and Duties

ALCOHOLIC BEVERAGES

Selectmen as licensing authority. Selectmen are the local licensing authority for the sale of alcoholic liquors in towns not having a licensing board or commission established under special statute.

Licenses. The selectmen, with the approval of the state Alcoholic Beverages Control Commission, issue licenses for the sale of beverages to be consumed on the premises. They also license the sale of such beverages to be consumed off the premises. Selectmen set the license fee within limits fixed by statute. Licenses also are issued for taverns in towns where these are authorized. No license shall be issued to any applicant who has been convicted on a federal or state narcotics charge.

Referendum on tavern sales. Selectmen are required to call a special election for a referendum on the question of licensing the sale of alcoholic beverages in taverns within 60 days after receiving a petition by one per cent of the voters. When a regular town election is about to be held, the vote is to be at that election if the petition is filed at least 30 days before the date of the election. The quesion is not to be submitted to the voters more frequently than once in two years.

Special licenses. Special licenses for the sale of beer and wine may be issued to the responsible manager of an indoor or outdoor activity or enterprise.

Pharmacy sales. Registered pharmacists holding a certificate of fitness from the state Board of Registration in Pharmacy may sell alcoholic beverages on prescription of a physician. A record book of such sales must be kept by the pharmacist and must be open at all times to inspection by the selectmen and their police officers. This type of sale is authorized irrespective of any town vote affecting the sale of alcoholic beverages. The selectmen have power to revoke or suspend for cause a pharmacist's certificate of fitness, but only after a hearing.

Registered pharmacists in towns where the sale of alcoholic beverages is authorized may be licensed by the selectmen to sell alcoholic beverages for medicinal, mechanical or chemical purposes without a physician's prescription. Such sales must also be recorded, and the books must be open to inspection at all times. Sales of this nature may be made only during regular local package store hours.

A registered pharmacist serving no food in his establishment may also be licensed under the standard procedure for regular package sales, but any such license would be included in the local quota of permits.

Seasonal licenses. The number of licenses in a town is set according to population, but towns having an increased temporary population during various times of the year are authorized additional seasonal licenses.

Control of licensed places. Selectmen may refuse to issue or renew a license for non-compliance with requirements. Following a hearing, they may modify, suspend, revoke or cancel any license issued. Selectmen may order a person holding a license not to sell or deliver alcoholic beverages for a period of three days in case of riot or great public excitement.

Authority of commission. The state Alcoholic Beverages Control Commission is authorized to adopt regulations relating to alcoholic beverages. A current copy of these regulations should be consulted by the selectmen. Local licensing authorities are required to file a report with the state commission after the close of each license year, containing the established schedule of fees and other information.

BOUNDARIES

Review of boundary lines. The boundary lines of every town are to be perambulated and the marks renewed once every five years by two or more of the selectmen or substitutes appointed in writing by the selectmen. The proceedings are to be recorded in the town records.

Notice of perambulation. The selectmen of the older of two towns are to give written notice to the selectmen of the other town of the time and place of meeting ten days in advance of the perambulation.

Notice to towns in other states. In towns bordering on another state, the selectmen are to give notice of their intention to perambulate the lines to the other town officers concerned. If the proposal is accepted, the perambulation is to be made.

Boundary markers. The selectmen of adjoining towns are to erect permament stone monuments at every angle of the boundary lines and crossing of highways. The expense is shared by both towns.

BUILDING INSPECTION

Building inspector. In towns having a building code the selectmen designate an inspector of buildings. Selectmen in towns accepting the chapter of law relating to tenement houses in towns are required to appoint a building inspector each year.

Request for state inspection. The selectmen may call upon an inspector of the Division of Inspection in the state Department of Public Safety to inspect any dangerous building or condition.

Fireproofing requirements. Towns accepting certain sections of state law may require buildings in certain areas to be constructed of incombustible materials, except detached houses more than 100 feet from other buildings, wooden structures erected on wharves and other places granted a license by the selectmen. A building erected other than as provided may be declared a common nuisance, and the selectmen may remove it in the same manner as a board of health may remove nuisances.

Survey of premises. If the owner, lessor or mortgagee in possession of an unsafe structure neglects or refuses to comply with requirements for its repair or removal, a survey of the premises is to be made by a board consisting of a surveyor, the head of the fire department and one disinterested person appointed by the inspector of buildings. If the town has no head of a fire department, the selectmen are to designate the officer to serve on such a board.

Plumbing inspection. The board of health may adopt rules and regulations for plumbing inspection which are formulated by the Board of State Examiners of Plumbers. Within 30 days the board of health is to appoint a plumbing inspector for a term of three years. Two or more towns may unite in forming a plumbing inspection district with expenses to be divided as agreed upon by the respective boards of health.

CIVIL DEFENSE

Local organization. Towns are required to establish a local organization for civil defense. A director, appointed by the manager of towns having a town manager and by the selectmen of other towns, is in charge of the unit. He is responsible for the organization, administration and operation of the local organization, subject to the direction and control of the appointing authority. The director may be a selectman.

Auxiliary units. Selectmen are to appoint, train and equip auxiliary firemen and auxiliary police. They also may establish other public protection units approved by the state Division of Civil Defense. Auxiliary workers and units are to be unpaid volunteers.

Aid to other towns. In the event of an emergency, and upon request, selectmen may authorize the town police department to aid another city or town in suppressing riots or violence. This assistance is to be given subject to such terms and conditions as may be prescribed by vote of the selectmen.

For the laws concerning civil defense, reference should be made to chapter 639 of the Acts of 1950 as amended, and to the executive order pertaining to civil defense.

COASTAL WATERS

Landing places. Selectmen of shore towns shall maintain at least one common landing place which is not to extend below the low water mark. They may provide additional landing places on petition of ten or more voters. They also may make rules and regulations relating to landing places and may appoint a custodian for them.

Construction on rivers and shore. The state Department of Public Works grants licenses for the construction or extension of a wharf, pier, dam, sea wall, road, bridge, structure, pipe line, conduit or cable in, over, under or upon a river, stream or tide water, or for the filling of land, making of excavations or driving of piles. Before such a license is issued, the state department is to give notice to the selectmen of the town where the work is to be performed in order that they may be heard.

Protection against erosion. A petition may be filed by the selectmen for enforcement by the Superior Court of a prohibition against the removal of stones, gravel, sand or other material which furnishes protection against erosion on land bordering on the sea.

Fences on waters. Selectmen may order a fence erected along a canal or waterway after a public hearing. If the order is not complied with, the fence may be built by the town at the expense of the person responsible.

Charles River bridges. The selectmen of towns bordering on the Charles River are required to give their consent to the rebuilding of any bridge across the river in their towns by the Metropolitan District Commission.

Fish traps. The selectmen of towns on coastal waters may authorize a person in writing to construct weirs, pound nets or fish traps in tidewater locations where no harbor lines exist or beyond harbor lines within the limits of the town for a period not exceeding five years, subject to such conditions as the selectmen determine. The authority given by the selectmen is not valid without the written approval of the state Department of Public Works and the director of the Division of Marine Fisheries, subject to such conditions as they may impose.

Coastal fisheries. Selectmen of coastal towns, when authorized by the town, may exercise control over coastal fisheries within the town. They may regulate or prohibit the taking of eels and shellfish, grant permits, make regulations and declare a closed season for any shellfish. They also may issue licenses to plant, grow, dig and take shellfish for not more than five years.

Shellfish constables. The selectmen may designate one or more constables in the town as shellfish constables for the detection of violations of shellfish laws and regulations.

Polluted areas. The selectmen or a town manager may request the state Department of Public Health to make an examination of coastal waters and flats and of shellfish in such waters to determine if they are contaminated.

Shellfish purification plant. The selectmen or 10 per cent of the voters in a town where coastal waters are polluted may petition the state for construction or maintenance of a shellfish purification plant. Such a plant may be operated by the state or by the town in which it is located, and the expense is apportioned among the cities and towns served in the proportion to which they contribute to the pollution.

Shore reservations. The annual town meeting of a town bordering on tidewater may instruct the selectmen to petition the county commissioners in writing for the establishment of a shore reservation on behalf of the county. The selectmen may agree in writing on behalf of the town to indemnify the county for any claims for damages to the extent authorized by the town meeting. They also may offer to contribute money, labor or materials for the project if this has been voted by the town meeting.

DISTRICTS

Airport district. Two or more cities and towns may establish a joint airport by vote of the town meeting in the respective towns. The selectmen are to meet within 30 days to draft a tentative agreement which must be approved by the state Director of Accounts and state Aeronautics Commission. The agreement is to include provisions for establishing a joint airport commission. This is described in the law as a joint enterprise rather than as a district.

Building inspection district. Two or more municipalities, by vote of the city council or town meeting, may form a building inspection district and appoint a joint inspector of buildings. The inspector is to be named by a comittee consisting of the mayor of a city and the chairman of the selectmen of each town in the district. The committee is to determine the relative amount of service to be performed in each city or town and apportion the amount of salary and expenses to be paid by each. A city or town may withdraw from such a district by a vote taken not less than 60 days before the end of any fiscal year.

The building inspector is the authorized representative of the Commissioner of Public Safety for the enforcement of laws relating to places of public assembly. In towns not having a building inspector or similar officer and which are not in a building inspection district, the selectmen are the authorized representatives.

Children's health camp district. Two or more municipalities may vote to form a union children's health camp district for a period of not more than five years. An unpaid commission on union children's health camps is to be in charge of such a district. Town members of the commission are chairmen of selectmen, with no vote, superintendents of schools, members of the board of health, and not more than ten residents of each town elected for the duration of the agreement by the ex-officio members.

Public beach district. Two or more adjoining municipalities may vote to form a public beach district for acquiring beaches. The district is to be under the control of a commission appointed by a joint committee consisting of the mayor and council president of each city and the chairman of the selectmen in each town.

Public welfare district. Two or more towns, with the approval of the state Commissioner of Public Welfare, may vote to form a public welfare district. The district is to employ suitable persons for assisting the board of public welfare or the selectmen acting as a board of public welfare. Employees of the district are to be appointed by a district welfare committee composed of one member from each town elected by and from the board of public welfare or selectmen acting as such a board.

Regional health district. Two or more municipalities may vote to form a regional health district, to consist of a regional board of health and a director of health. The board is to have at least one member from each municipality. The town meeting may choose the method of selecting the member from the town. The town member may be appointed by the selectmen, appointed by the board of health, elected by the town meeting or chosen by any other method decided upon by the town meeting.

Regional planning district. Under a regional planning law adopted in 1955, any group of municipalities may vote to become members of a regional planning district, with the approval of the Division of Planning in the state Department of Commerce. There is no reference in the law to the duties of selectmen.

Regional school district. Upon recommendation of a regional school district planning committee that a regional school district be formed, selectmen are to submit the question to an annual or special town meeting held within 30 days after receiving the recommendations.

A regional school district is to submit an annual report with a financial statement and other information desired by the district school committee or selectmen. The Director of Accounts audits a regional school district and sends a copy of the audit report to the selectmen of each town in the district.

Notice of the amount of any debt authorized by the district school committee shall be given to selectmen of each town in the district within seven days. Town meeting may vote disapproval within 30 days.

Transportation area. Two or more municipalities may unite to establish a transportation area for the operation of passenger and freight service on street railways. The area is to constitute a body corporate and politic upon approval of the voters and the state Department of Public Utilities.

A town, by vote of its selectmen, may make preliminary agreements with a street railway company for the lease or purchase and for the operation of the company's properties. Upon approval by ballot at a town meeting called for the purpose, the agreement is binding, and the selectmen have authority to execute such further agreements as are necessary to give effect to the purposes of the preliminary agreement. The management and control of a transportation area is vested in a board of trustees, two of whom are chosen by the selectmen of each town concerned.

Veterans' services district. Two or more adjoining municipalities, only one of which is a city, may form a district for the furnishing of veterans' services by vote of the selectmen. A district board composed of the mayor of a city and the chairman of the selectmen of each town is in charge of the district. The board may employ a director of veterans' services if they believe such an officer is necessary. There also is an unpaid advisory board of from five to 15 members appointed by the district board. Expenses of the district are apportioned on the basis of the assessed valuation of each municipality. The treasurer of one of the cities or towns serves as treasurer of the district. A town may withdraw at the end of any fiscal year on 60 days notice.

Wire inspection district. Two or more municipalities may vote to form a district for the appointment of an inspector of wires. His compensation is paid by each municipality as the city and town members of the district determine.

DOGS

Appointment of dog officers. The selectmen are to designate one or more dog officers each year and report their names to the county commissioners. They may be police officers or constables. Instead of appointing a dog officer, selectmen may enter into a contract for such services with a domestic charitable organization incorporated for the purpose of protecting animals from cruelty, neglect or abuse. The contract is subject to the approval of the county commissioners.

Complaints concerning dogs. Selectmen are to investigate the complaint of any person relating to a vicious or annoying dog and take any necessary action. They may allow the owner of such a dog seven days to give bond of $200 on the condition that he restrain the dog for 12 months following action by the selectmen.

Damage done by dogs. A person suffering a loss by reason of injury or damage done by dogs to livestock or fowl may inform the chairman of the selectmen or any of the selectmen, whose duty it is to appraise the damage if it does not exceed $50. If the damage is more than $50 the appraisal is to be made by three persons: a selectman, a person appointed by the one alleged to have suffered damage and the third to be selected by the other two. The selectman is to send a certificate of damage to the county treasurer within ten days after the appraisal. The county commissioners may investigate, summon the appraisers and issue an order to the treasurer for the payment of a just claim.

Investigation by county. The county commissioners are to appoint persons to investigate damage done by dogs. They are to investigate any such damage in a town at the request of the selectmen.

Restraining of dogs. The selectmen may order dogs to be muzzled or restrained from running at large during stated times and may send certified copies of such an order to owners and keepers of dogs. They may offer a reward up to $25 for a dog killing livestock or fowl and may take action against the owner.

Complaint concerning kennels. Within seven days after the filing of a petition with the selectmen by 25 persons annoyed by a dog kennel, the selectmen are to give notice of a hearing to be held within 14 days after the notice. Within seven days after the hearing, the selectmen report their recommendations in writing to the county commissioners, except in Nantucket and Suffolk counties. The county commissioners investigate within seven days after receiving the report and either may take action on the complaint or dismiss the petition.

Unlicensed dogs. Selectmen are required to order the dog officer to catch and confine unlicensed dogs within ten days after the first of June and prosecute a complaint against the owners. Such dogs are to be kept in a sanitary place, a licensed kennel, or by the S. P. C. A. and may be sold or otherwise disposed of if not licensed.

ELECTIONS

Regulations. Selectmen may make regulations relative to the use of ballot boxes and the receiving, counting and return of ballots.

Registrars of voters. Every town is required to have a board of registrars of voters, consisting of the town clerk and three other persons appointed in writing by the selectmen to serve for three year overlapping terms. Registrars of voters are to be appointed so that the members shall represent the two leading political parties.

Board of election commissioners. By accepting a section of law, a town may establish a board of election commissioners. The board is to consist of four members apppointed by the selectmen for four year terms beginning in April. Two of the members are to represent each one of the major political parties. The board of registrars of voters becomes the election board until the terms of its members expire, but if the town clerk is a member the selectmen are to appoint a new member in his place. The board selects its own chairman and secretary. If the members are unable to agree, the designation of a chairman and secretary is made by the selectmen.

Duties of board. The board of election commissioners has all the powers and duties of a board of registrars of voters and all those of the selectmen and town clerk relating to caucuses, primaries and elections, except for giving notice of elections and fixing the days and hours of elections.

Establishment of voting precincts. A town may direct the selectmen to divide the town into voting precincts. If so directed the selectmen are to file a report within 60 days, accompanied by a map and description of the precincts and a statement of the number of voters in each area at the time of the preceding election. If the report is rejected by the town meeting, the town at any time may direct that it be done again.

Changes in voting precincts. A town meeting may make any changes in voting precincts which the selectmen recommend and which are filed with the town clerk seven days before the meeting. Only those changes may be made which are recommended by the selectmen.

Division in towns with elected meeting members. In a town in which the town meeting members are elected, a voting precinct may be divided. If this is done the seletmen are to notify each voter within 20 days.

Map or description of precincts. When a town is divided into voting precincts, or when precincts are changed, the selectmen are to post a map or description in the office of the town clerk and three public places in each precinct. They also are to furnish copies to the registrars of voters, assessors and election officers.

Precinct election officers. The selectmen of towns divided into voting precincts are to appoint election officers for each precinct between July 15 and August 15 of each year. These are a warden, deputy warden, clerk, deputy clerk, two inspectors and two deputy inspectors. Selectmen may also appoint two additional inspectors and two additional deputy inspectors.

Party representation. The election officers are to be appointed so that the two major political parties will have equal representation. Two of the election officers may be persons not representing either party, but the others must be equally divided between the two parties. The warden must be of a different party from the clerk and not more than half of the inspectors are to be of the same party. Vacanies must be filled so as to preserve the equal party representation. The principal officer and his deputy, however, must be of the same political party.

Submission of party lists. The chairman of each political party committtee is to file with the selectmen by the first day of June in each year a list of his party members who desire appointment as election officers. The list is to contain not more than eight names for each place to be filled. Supplemental lists may be submitted for the filling of vacancies. If a party chairman fails to provide a list within 15 days after being notified by the selectmen in writing before June 15, the selectmen may appoint the party members without a list. The selectmen after five days notice may conduct examinations of persons whose names appear on the lists. The party chairman may be present at the examination.

Designation of polling places. The selectmen of towns having voting precincts are to designate the polling places for each precinct at least 20 days before a state election and ten days before a special election. They also are to have the polling places prepared for voting. When a polling place in a precinct is changed from one location to another, the selectmen are to have printed descriptions posted in public places in the precinct or are to notify each voter by mail.

Removal of election officers. An election officer may be removed by the selectmen upon a written charge of incompetence preferred by the town clerk or by six voters of the voting precinct concerned.

Powers of selectmen in towns without precincts. In towns not divided into voting precincts, the selectmen at state elections have the powers of wardens in cities or moderators in towns. They are to act through their chairman or senior member present, who is the presiding election officer.

Ballot clerks in towns without precincts. In towns without voting precincts where official ballots are used, the selectmen are to appoint two voters as ballot clerks at state elections before the opening of the polls. The selectmen or moderator presiding may oppoint additional ballot clerks and fill any vacancy. Not more than one may be appointed for every 400 voters or a major portion thereof.

Additional ballot boxes. At a state election or at a town election in a town using official ballots the selectmen may vote to have more than one ballot box used at any polling place. If more than one ballot box is used, the selectmen may divide the voting lists into as many sections as there are boxes. The Secretary of the Commonwealth is to provide additional ballot boxes at the expense of the town upon written request of the selectmen.

Hours of voting. The notices or warrants by the selectmen for the calling of an election in towns where official ballots are used are to specify the offices to be voted for and the time when the polls are to be opened and closed, within limits specified by statute.

Certification of election records. In towns divided into voting precincts, the selectmen and town clerk are required to examine copies of the records of election officers at state elections and certify all original and additional copies of the records, giving notice of errors for which corrections must be made. A penalty is provided by law for a selectman who wilfully signs or issues an election certificate which is not in accordance with the results of an election as shown by the records.

Notice of party caucus. The chairman or secretary of the town committee of a political party is to notify the selectmen at least two weeks in advance the date of the party caucus. The selectmen are required to provide polling places at the expense of the town and to notify the chairman or secretary of their location at least ten days previous to the date of the caucus. The selectmen must arrange the polling places in such a manner as to permit voting in two or more lines if requested in writing not later than 12 days before the caucus by 25 voters.

Holding of town caucus. A town using official ballots may vote at any annual meeting to hold a town caucus, called by the selectmen, for the nonpartisan nomination of candidates for town officers. The two persons receiving the highest number of votes at a town caucus are declared nominated. After the expiration of three years, a town may rescind such a vote at a meeting held 60 days before the annual town meeting.

Vacancies in elective offices. If there is a vacancy in the office of representative in Congress, the Governor issues a precept to the selectmen directing them to call an election. If the vacancy is in the office of state representative, the Speaker of the House of Representatives issues a precept to the selectmen. For vacancies in the positions of county treasurer or county register of deeds, the county commissioners issue a precept, except in Suffolk and Nantucket counties. When there is a vacancy in the county commissioners, the board of examiners issues a precept to the selectmen.

Voting machines. A town may vote to purchase or lease voting machines at a meeting held at least 90 days before a primary or election at which they are to be used. Voting machines are to be used at all primaries and elections thereafter until otherwise ordered by the selectmen.

FINANCE

Appropriations. A town is authorized to appropriate money for the exercise of any of its corporate powers, including numerous specific purposes which are described by law.

Finance committee. Every town in which valuation for the purpose of apportioning the state tax exceeds $1 million is required to provide for the election or appointment of an appropriation, advisory or finance committee. It is the duty of the committee to consider any or all municipal questions for the purpose of making reports or recommendations to the town.

Other towns with a lesser valuation may provide for such a committee by vote of the town.

Town budget. The finance committee submits the budget at the annual town meeting unless the selectmen are authorized to do so under the town by-laws. In towns not having a finance committee it is submitted by the selectmen.

Transfers of appropriations. On recommendation of the appropriation, advisory or finance committee or of the selectmen in a town not having such a committee, any town meeting may vote to transfer an amount previously appropriated to any other use authorized by law.

Reserve fund. A town may appropriate a reserve fund for extraordinary expenditures not exceeding five per cent of the tax levy of the preceding year. Transfers from the fund may be voted by the finance committee or by the selectmen in towns not having such a committee.

Overlay reserve. The balance remaining in an overlay reserve, added to the total of assessments to cover abatements, is transferred to a reserve fund for extraordinary or unforeseen expenses.

Exceeding appropriations. No town department is permitted by law to incur liability in excess of its appropriation except by a vote of two-thirds of the selectmen in cases of extreme emergency involving the health or safety of persons or property. Each item voted by the town meeting is considered as a separate appropriation.

Estimates of appropriations. Town officers, including the selectmen, are to furnish the town accountant, if any, detailed estimates of the amounts necessary for accounts under their jurisdiction for the ensuing year. The estimates are to be submitted not less than ten days before the end of the financial year. If there is no town accountant, the information is given to the appropriation, advisory or finance committee. If there is no such committee, it is given to the selectmen. The selectmen in towns without such a committee designate the amounts which they think should be appropriated for the ensuing year.

Fees of town officers. A town may adopt a by-law requiring town officers to pay all of their fees into the town treasury or to report the amount of their fees to the selectmen. Selectmen are to publish such information in the annual town report.

Cemetery funds. A town may receive gifts and bequests for maintaining cemeteries. The town treasurer is to invest such funds according to the stipulations and as ordered by the selectmen and cemetery commissioners.

Printing of recommended appropriations. It is the duty of selectmen to print and distribute copies of recommended appropriations before the annual town meeting.

Inspection of accounts. All town accounts are subject to inspection by selectmen. They may require any person presenting a claim against the town to make an oath as to its accuracy.

Approval of bills and payrolls. Selectmen are required to approve all bills or payrolls before they are paid by the treasurer. They may refuse approval in whole or in part as fraudulent, unlawful or excessive and give the treasurer written reasons for refusal.

Report of irregularities. The town auditors are required to report any fraud or irregularity in trust accounts to the selectmen and treasurer.

Expenses of selectmen. Selectmen are to approve and transmit to the town accountant, at least once each month, any bills and payrolls of their office.

Exhausting of appropriations. Whenever an appropriation has been expended or when it appears that liabilities may exceed the unexpended balance, the town accountant in towns having an accountant is to send a statement to the selectmen at least once a month showing the orders approved, warrants drawn and balance of each appropriation.

Liability insurance. A town may provide liability insurance for drivers of motor vehicles, including volunteer drivers of town fire apparatus, whose services in such a capacity are approved by the selectmen.

Advertising town. Appropriations for advertising the town, for which additional amounts must be raised by public subscription, are spent under the direction of the selectmen.

Highway safety program. Selectmen supervise the spending of money for any highway safety program for which an appropriation is made.

Disaster relief. Selectmen are to have charge of the spending of any appropriation for the purpose of providing food, shelter and other necessaries of life to the people of the town in time of war, emergency or distress.

Sinking fund records. The records and securities of sinking fund commissioners are available for the inspection of the selectmen or any town committee authorized for the purpose.

Trust funds. Selectmen in towns under 5,000 population accepting a permissive section of the statutes may act as commissioners of trust funds until the town population exceeds that figure.

Violation of finance laws. The selectmen or any five taxpayers may report a violation of the finance laws to the district attorney for investigation and prosecution.

Appropriation for unpaid bills. A town may appropriate money for unpaid bills of previous years by a four-fifths vote of the annual town meeting or by a nine-tenths vote of a special town meeting if certificates have been filed with the selectmen stating that the goods or services were ordered by a town official or employee and were delivered or rendered to the town.

Special tax collectors. If town taxes remain uncollected at the end of three years and recovery cannot be made on the bond of the tax collector, the selectmen are to appoint a collector of taxes for the current year or a special collector of taxes.

Accounts of collector. The selectmen may require a tax collector to show them a record of all money received and to present treasurer's receipts once in two months.

Removal of collector. The selectmen may remove a tax collector if he becomes insane, absconds, removes from town, refuses to exhibit his books or is unable to discharge his duty.

Custodian of tax reverted property. The selectmen of a town which holds property acquired by foreclosure of tax titles may appoint a custodian to have the management and control of such property. The custodian, with the approval of the selectmen, may lease the property for not more than three years if he thinks that sale of the property is not practicable at the time.

Request for state audit. Selectmen may petition the state Director of Accounts for an audit of town accounts whenever they consider that conditions warrant such action. Upon completion of the audit, a report and suggestions are to be made to the selectmen.

Annual audit. The state Director of Accounts is required to have an annual audit made of all towns and report to the selectmen. He also may investigate the accounts and financial transactions of any town officer, department, board or commission and report to the selectmen.

Compensation by special district. The amounts appropriated by a fire, water or improvement district as compensation for a town assessor or collector in performing services for the district is to be not less than an amount determined by the selectmen and the prudential committee of the district. In the case of a water district not having a prudential committee, the amount is decided by the selectmen and water commissioners. If the selectmen and the committee or commissioners cannot agree, the amount is fixed by the Commissioner of Corporations and Taxation.

Signing of bonds and notes. Bonds and notes issued by a town, within limitations prescribed by the chapter of the state laws dealing with municipal finance, are to be signed by the town treasurer and a majority of the selectmen.

Interest rate. Bonds, notes and other securities issued by towns are to bear such a rate of interest as may be fixed by the town treasurer with approval of the selectmen.

Signing of notes. Notes issued by the town are to be signed by the treasurer, and a majority of the selectmen are required to countersign each note in the presence of the town clerk. The clerk shall so certify on the note and affix the town seal.

Borrowing outside debt limit. The town treasurer, with approval of the selectmen, may incur debt outside of the debt limit for highway construction and issue notes for one year in anticipation of state or county reimbursements.

Borrowing on notes. The town treasurer, with approval of a majority of the selectmen, may borrow on notes during any one month between the first day of January and the date of the next annual town meeting a sum not exceeding one-twelfth of the amount obtained by adding the previous tax levy and the sum received from the state income tax in the previous year.

Betterments. Assessments for betterments may be made whenever a limited area receives a benefit or advantage for a public improvement other than the general advantage to the community. The chapters of law relating to betterments should be consulted.

Parking meters. A town may appropriate money for parking meters and may vote to authorize a town board or officer to enter into an agreement for their acquisition, installation and maintenance.

FIRE DEPARTMENT

Town fire department. Towns accepting certain sections of law may establish a fire department under the control of a chief appointed by the selectmen and who may be removed by them for cause after a hearing. The chief has full authority over the department and makes the rules and regulations. He purchases property and apparatus and fixes the compensation of firemen with approval of the selectmen. This does not affect the tenure of office or apply to the removal of members of fire departments in towns under civil service.

Commissioner of public safety. A town may vote to have the selectmen appoint a commissioner of public safety who shall be both the fire chief and police chief. This office is discussed under the heading of police department.

Assistance to other towns. The selectmen may authorize the fire department to give aid and assistance to any city, town or fire district in the state or in an adjoining state, subject to such conditions and restrictions as they may prescribe. The town by-laws also may provide for such situations.

Organization of fire district. If a town meeting declines to provide fire protection for a particular area which has requested it, the residents of the area may propose that a fire district be established. When the organization of a fire district is proposed, on petition of seven freeholders the selectmen are required to call a meeting of the inhabitants of the proposed district in the same manner as for a town meeting. If the selectmen decline to do so, a justice of peace may call the meeting.

Firewards and enginemen. Under the provisions of old laws in existence for many years, the selectmen may appoint firewards, enginemen, engineers and enginemen for private engines.

Associations of firemen. No association, society or club organized as firemen is to be established in any town except by written permission of the selectmen.

Forest warden. The selectmen are to appoint a forest warden in June of each year for a term of one year and notify the director of Forests and

Parks in the state Department of Natural Resources of the appointment. The same person may be a forest warden and a selectman, tree warden or chief of the fire department. If the selectmen fail to appoint a forest warden in June, or within 30 days after a vacancy, the state Director of Forests and Parks is required to notify them to fill the position. If they fail to comply within 14 days, the state director may make the appointment.

Payments for forest fires. Payment is to be made to forest wardens, their deputies and to persons assisting them at forest fires, as well as for property used at a forest fire under their direction. The rate of payment may be fixed by the town meeting, but if this has not been done it is determined by the selectmen. Money appropriated by a town for the prevention of forest fires is spent by the forest warden under the supervision of the selectmen.

Fire chief as forest warden. The chief of the fire department may act as forest warden with the right to appoint deputy forest wardens, subject to the approval of the selectmen.

Licensing authority. The selectmen are defined as the local licensing authority under the chapter of state laws relating to fire prevention.

FIRE PREVENTION

Manufacture of fireworks. A building is not to be used for the manufacture of fireworks and firecrackers without a license from the selectmen and a permit from the state Fire Marshal.

Inflammable materials. Rules and regulations relating to the use, storage, handling, manufacture and sale of petroleum products, explosives, fireworks and other inflammable materials are made by the state Board of Fire Prevention Regulations. Towns also may adopt by-laws pertaining to these things. A building is not to be used for these purposes unless the selectmen have granted a license for such use of the land on which the building is situated. The license application is to have an endorsement of approval or disapproval by the head of the fire department. A license may be granted by the selectmen subject to the conditions and restrictions they may impose, following a hearing with seven days notice which is advertised at the expense of the applicant. Such a license is a grant attaching to the land as an incident of ownership and not a personal privilege. These provisions do not apply to private garages for three automobiles or less.

Bond for storage of fireworks. A bond of not less than $10,000, in such amount as the selectmen determine with approval of the state Fire Marshal, is required for the storage of fireworks in quantities in any building located within 1,000 feet of an inhabited building or place of assembly, except as provided by the state Board of Fire Prevention Regulations.

GENERAL ADMINISTRATION

Election of selectmen. The annual town meeting is required to choose by ballot three or five selectmen for terms of one or three years. If a town which elects selectmen for one year votes that they shall perform the duties of any specified officers which the town meeting is privileged to elect, the town shall provide at the next annual town meeting for the election of selectmen for three year overlapping terms. Those elected are required to take an oath of office as selectmen.

Vacancies in office of selectman. If there is a vacancy in the office of selectman or a failure to elect a selectman, the remaining selectmen may call a special election to fill the vacancy. They are required to call a special election for the purpose if a request in writing is made by 200 voters or 20 per cent of the total voters in the town, whichever number is the lesser, and such request is filed not less than 100 days before the next annual election.

Census. The selectmen are required to have a decennial census of the town conducted in 1925 and every tenth year thereafter, under the supervision of the Secretary of the Commonwealth. For this purpose the selectmen may use the services of the police and registrars of voters.

County reports. The annual report of the county commissioners is required to be sent to the selectmen of each town in the county. The selectmen may request the state Director of Accounts for a copy of the annual report of county finances which is submitted to the legislature.

Date of settlement. If there is a question as to the date of settlement of a town for the purpose of celebrating a town anniversary, it is to be determined by the selectmen with approval of the voters.

Eminent domain. The selectmen may purchase or take by eminent domain any land, easement or right for any municipal purpose not otherwise authorized by statute, if approved by vote of the town and appropriation has been made by a two-thirds vote of the town meeting. Where no other provision is made by law, the taking of land by eminent domain by or on behalf of a town is to be made by the selectmen. Such takings are authorized for numerous specific purposes by the selectmen or other officers. Readers are referred to the chapters of law on eminent domain and judicial proceedings for eminent domain and betterments. (See G.L., chapters 79, 80 and 80A.)

Executive secretary. A town may provide by by-law or vote to authorize the selectmen to appoint an executive secretary for a term of one or three years, who may be removed by the selectmen at their discretion. The executive secretary is not to hold an elective office, but he may be appointed by the selectmen to any other town position. He also may be appointed by any other town officer or board to another town position with approval of the selectmen. He is to act by and for the selectmen in any matter assigned to him and with their approval may perform such other duties as may be requested of him by any other town officer, board or committee.

Investigation of town departments. Selectmen of any town may make an investigation into the conduct and operation of any town department. Upon completion of such investigation a report shall be submitted to the town clerk. This report shall be printed in the annual town report.

Jurors. Selectmen are to prepare a list of persons qualified to serve as jurors before the first day of July in each year. The jury list is to be printed annually before the first day of August and a copy delivered to the selectmen. The selectmen are to have the names on the jury list placed separately in a ballot box kept by the town clerk. Jurors are selected by drawing ballots from the box. When jurors are to be drawn, the town clerk and selectmen are to meet at the office of the town clerk or some other public place. If the town clerk is absent, the selectmen may proceed without him. One of the selectmen is to draw from the box a number of ballots equal to the number of jurors required. A town may vote to have the drawing made in open town meeting.

Open meetings. All meetings of every public body, however appointed, elected or constituted shall be open to the public and the press except when it is voted to go into executive session. An executive session may be held only to discuss and vote on matters affecting the public security, the reputation of any person, or the financial interest of the local government. Executive sessions are not authorized for meetings conducted to investigate any board or agency of a municipal government, or to investigate any legislation proposing to alter the existing local governmental structure.

Except in an emergency at least 24 hours notice must be given of any meeting of any public body. Accurate records of all meetings and action taken, including executive sessions, must be maintained.

If the public or press is denied access to any meeting or session, ten registered voters may seek an order from the courts directing the public officials concerned to open their meetings and records of meetings.

Parking areas. A town may acquire off-street parking areas by purchase, gift, eminent domain or lease not to exceed five years. Meter receipts may be applied toward the cost of acquiring and maintaining the area.

Public Markets. The town clerk is required to certify to the chairman of the selectmen the sufficiency of a petition filed by 5 per cent of the voters for the designation of a public market place.

Service of process. In an action against a county, city, town, parish or religious society or against the incorporated proprietors of wharves, general fields or real estate lying in common, service is to be made upon the treasurer, but if no treasurer is found it may be made upon one of the county commissioners, the town clerk or one of the selectmen.

Town report. The selectmen, at the expense of the town, are required to print an annual town report before the town meeting. It must include the report of the selectmen, the school committee and other officers and must contain the jury list.

War memorial. Towns which appropriate money or accept gifts for a war memorial may provide for a board of trustees to have charge of the construction and to be responsible for its care and maintenance. The board is to consist of the chairman of the selectmen and five members elected by the town meeting. Two of the members must not be veterans. Vacancies are filled by the remaining members of the board. When first established, the selectmen may appoint a temporary board to serve until the next annual town meeting.

Witnesses. Witnesses may be summoned to attend, testify and produce books and papers at a hearing before the selectmen and certain boards specified in the statute as to matters within their authority. Such witnesses are to be summoned in the same manner, paid the same fee and subject to the same penalties for default as witnesses in civil cases before the courts.

GRADE CROSSINGS

Alteration of railroad crossing. The selectmen may apply to the county commissioners for the alteration of a railroad crossing, approaches or a bridge at such a crossing. The county commissioners after a hearing decide if the alteration is necessary and certify their decision to interested parties and to the state Department of Public Utilities.

Determination of expense. A commission of three disinterested persons determines which party shall carry the decision into effect and assume the expense of alteration and future upkeep. Unless the parties concerned are in agreement, the commission may apportion the expense among the railroad, county and town. If a state highway is involved, the state may be included in the apportionment.

Application to court. Unless those concerned are in agreement, the selectmen, state Department of Public Utilities, state Department of Public Works or any party in interest may apply to the Superior Court, and the court may appoint such a commission after notice and hearing.

Appeal for jury decision. The selectmen or other parties in interest may appeal to the Superior Court for revision by a jury within 14 days after the making of an award by the commission. The selectmen, or other party designated to carry such a decision into effect, may recover in contract from any other party the portion awarded to be paid.

Abolition of grade crossing. The state Department of Public Works receives petitions from selectmen for abolition of a grade crossing. After a hearing, the crossing may be placed on a list of those suggested for abolition to the state Department of Public Utilities. The Department of Public Utilities, after a hearing, designates a recommended program of grade crossing abolition.

Agreement on crossing changes. If the selectmen and the directors of a railroad corporation agree that an alteration should be made in a grade crossing, approaches or bridge at a crossing or that a crossing be discontinued, an agreement in writing is signed by the chairman of the selectmen if authorized by vote of the town. The agreement requires approval of the state Department of Public Utilities after a notice and hearing. The state Department of Public Works may join in the agreement and it may decide that the state shall share in the expense. The provisions relative to applications made to county commissioners do not apply to cases discussed in this paragraph.

Repair of railroad bridges. The selectmen may apply to the state Department of Public Utilities to require the maintenance and repair of a railroad bridge. The state department, after notice and hearing, may decide that the work is necessary and may prescribe the manner in which it will be done.

Crossing changes by railroad. A railroad corporation may raise or lower a highway to permit the railroad to pass over or under it, after obtaining a decree from the county commissioners prescribing the alterations and giving security for compliance to the town. The Supreme Judicial Court may enjoin the railroad corporation if it acts without obtaining a decree or giving security.

New railroad crossing highway. If a railroad is laid out across a highway, on application of the selectmen and after notice and hearing, the county commissioners may authorize a crossing at the same level with approval of the state Department of Public Works. In the case of a state highway, the application is made to the state Department of Public Works.

New highway crossing railroad. A local highway may be laid out across an existing railroad with approval of the county commissioners and the state Department of Public Works for a state highway.

Obstruction of highway by railroad. If a railroad crosses a highway so as to obstruct it instead of crossing over, under or at the same level, or if a railroad refuses or neglects to keep a bridge or other structure at a crossing in proper repair, the selectmen may notify the county commissioners. After a notice and hearing, the county commissioners may make a decree prescribing what repairs shall be made by the railroad and may order security for performance of the decree. A commission of three disinterested persons determines which party is to carry the decision into effect and which shall pay the cost and future expenses. The commission may apportion the cost among the parties.

Private railroads on highways. A private railroad for moving freight cannot be constructed on or across a local highway or other travelled place without the consent of the selectmen, or on a state highway without the consent of the state Department of Public Works.

Crossing abolition by street railway. With written approval of the selectmen, after notice to owners and a public hearing, a street railway company may take land by eminent domain for the abolition of a grade crossing. The selectmen may authorize structures which are necessary for carrying a street railway over or under a railroad. If a state highway is involved, the authority lies with the state Department of Public Works.

HEALTH

Board of health. A town elects three members of a board of health for terms of three years if the town provides for such a board. Otherwise the selectmen act as a board of health.

Inspector of health. If a town votes to have the selectmen act as a board of health, they may appoint an inspector of health to assist them with their duties. In towns of less than 3,000 population they may appoint the school physician as inspector of health.

Health department. Towns accepting certain sections of the statutes may create a health department with a commissioner of health and an advisory council to replace a board of health. The selectmen, if authorized by vote of the town meeting, appoint the commissioner of health for a five-year term. He is required to be a graduate of a medical school with four years full time experience or to have a degree in public health and two years experience. The advisory council consists of six members appointed by the selectmen for six year overlapping terms. Two of the members must be physicians.

Regional health district. Cities and towns may form regional health districts. These are discussed under "Districts."

Appeal from state department. An appeal from an order of the state Department of Health may be made to the Superior Court. Such notice as the court may order is given to the chairman of the selectmen.

Children's health camp. Towns accepting certain sections of law may establish children's health camps under the direction of an unpaid commission on children's health camps. The commission consists of the chairman of the selectmen with no vote, superintendent of schools, members of the board of health and seven residents of each town appointed by the chairman of the selectmen to serve for three year overlapping terms. One member is designated chairman of the commission by the chairman of the selectmen.

Children's health camp district. Cities and towns may form union children's health camp districts. These are discussed under "Districts."

Drinking water for employees. Industrial establishments, public garages, express and trucking companies are required to provide drinking water for employees. A complaint of violations may be made by the selectmen or board of health.

Garbage disposal and incineration. The selectmen, board of health or other officers may contract for garbage and rubbish disposal for not more than five years. If authorized by the town meeting and the Emergency Finance Board, they may also contract for garbage and rubbish incineration. The board of health approves the site of any dumping ground or incinerator but the selectmen may appeal to the state Department of Health from any health board decision as to site.

Slaughter houses. Regulation of slaughter houses is a public health function. A license to conduct a slaughter house or for a canning, salting, smoking or rendering establishment is issued by the selectmen or by the board of health in towns of more than 5,000 population having a board of health. A similar license is issued for places manufacturing sausage or chopped meat. Slaughtering is to be conducted only on specified days in the presence of an inspector of the board of health or the selectmen acting as a board of health. A license also is required for poultry slaughtering houses, but this does not apply to persons engaged in the production of poultry on their own farms.

HIGHWAYS

Highway officers. A town is to choose one or more highway surveyors for one or three years, or it may choose to elect a road commissioner for one year or three road commissioners for three years. If the town does not provide that they be elected by the town, they are appointed by the selectmen.

Highway surveyor. A highway surveyor has exclusive control of ordinary highway repairs without being subject to the authority of the selectmen. If a town has more than one highway surveyor, the selectmen are to assign to each of them the limits and divisions of the roads for which he is responsible.

Road commissioners. If a town votes to elect road commissioners, they have all the powers and duties of selectmen and highway surveyors relative to public ways, monuments, guide posts, sidewalks and shade trees.

Superintendent of streets. In a town not having a highway surveyor or road commissioners, the selectmen appoint a superintendent of streets if the town has voted to have a superintendent instead of the other highway officials. The superintendent has charge of highway repairs under the direction of the selectmen. The selectmen of two or more towns may unite in the appointment of a joint superintendent of streets with the approval of the state Department of Public Works.

Board of public works. If a town votes to establish a board of public works with authority to appoint a superintendent of public works, under an act of 1953, the board and superintendent are the successors of the previous highway officials of the town.

Laying out highways. The selectmen or road commissioners may lay out, relocate or alter town highways and order specific repairs to be made. They have original jurisdiction, concurrent with the county commissioners, on petitions for altering, relocating or making specific repairs on highways within the town.

Eminent domain. The selectmen or road commissioners, with the authority of the town meeting, may take land for highways by eminent domain, by purchase or otherwise, after seven days notice of their intention to owners of land to be taken and within 30 days after the town meeting at which it is authorized. They also may take any land necessary for securing or protecting a public highway.

Acceptance by town. A town highway which is laid out or relocated must be accepted by the town at a town meeting. In case of a refusal or delay on the part of a town in accepting a highway, any person may petition the county commissioners within one year, and they may give their approval with the same effect as though it were accepted by the town.

If the selectmen or road commissioners unreasonably refuse or neglect to lay out, relocate or alter a highway when requested in writing by one or more inhabitants, the county commissioners may do so after receiving a petition filed within one year.

A description of the location, boundaries and measurements of a highway which is laid out or relocated is to be filed with the town clerk prior to its acceptance by the town meeting.

Application for state highway. Selectmen may apply by written petition to the state Department of Public Works for the state to take over an existing highway or lay out a new highway in the town.

Contributions for state highways. The selectmen, road commissioners or other town highway officers, if authorized by vote of the town meeting, may agree in writing to contribute money, labor or materials toward the cost of a state highway in the town. The town also may contribute toward the cost of a state trail or path.

Contract with state. The state Department of Public Works may contract with a town for the maintenance and repair of a state highway in the town.

State assistance for local highways. The expenditure of state funds for the repair and improvement of highways, other than state highways, in towns with valuations of less than $5 million is made on written petition of the selectmen. The cost of snow removal and sanding, including the cost of renting trucks and equipment, may be paid from such amounts. The town valuations are those established by an act of 1945 for the purpose of apportioning the state tax. The towns contribute an amount based upon their road mileage according to a schedule fixed by law.

Highway mileage. The state Department of Public Works determines the number of miles of town highways entitled to benefits and notifies the selectmen of the amount of the town contribution required.

Contract for local highways. Towns may contract with the state Department of Public Works for the performance of work so authorized or the selectmen may request that the state have the work done by others, with the town paying its proportionate part of the expense.

County contribution. A county also may contribute funds for such repair or improvement of a local highway by agreement of the county commissioners with the selectmen and state department.

Authority of state department. The Department of Public Works may spend state money on a local highway as it deems best, either on its existing location or a new location established by the selectmen. The road does not become a state highway or a responsibility of the state because of such work.

Temporary repairs on certain private ways. Voters in annual town meeting may authorize temporary repairs to private roads which have been open to the public for six or more years. Such repairs, limited to filling holes in the sub-surface and repair of surface material, shall be made only after the selectmen secure agreements executed by all abutting owners to release the town from any damages caused by such repairs. These agreements must be recorded in the district registry of deeds.

Selectmen are authorized to assess betterments upon land owners benefiting from such repairs, a total of one-half of the entire cost apportioned on a frontage basis.

Maintenance by town. If a highway is constructed or improved with state money, it is the duty of the town to keep it in repair. The Department of Public Works may notify the selectmen of the repairs that are necessary. If local officials do not make the repairs the state department may have them made at the expense of the town.

Snow removal agreements. The selectmen, highway surveyor or other highway officer in towns which accept a particular section of the statutes may enter into agreements with other towns for snow and ice removal. A town is to be reimbursed from the regular highway and snow removal appropriations of the other town to which the service is rendered.

Snow removal from private ways. Towns accepting a permissive section of law may appropriate funds for the removal of snow and ice from private roads designated by the selectmen that are open to public use.

Snow removal expenses. The town officers in charge of highways, with the written approval of a majority of the selectmen, may incur additional liabilities for snow and ice removal to an authorized amount. This requires the approval of the appropriation, advisory or finance committee in towns having such a committee. In other towns it must be approved by the state Director of Accounts at the request of the selectmen.

Laying of pipes. Selectmen may authorize the laying of water pipes in highways on such terms and conditions as they prescribe. They may approve the laying of steam and hot water pipes for private use and may order their removal after notice and hearing. Pipes conveying petroleum products also may be authorized, subject to rules and regulations of the state Department of Public Safety. In towns accepting a section of the statutes, the selectmen, road commissioners or sewer commissioners may lay water and sewer pipes in a highway prior to the start of construction when a highway is to be established or changed.

Work on pipes in highways. A gas company may dig in a highway so far as necessary with written consent of the selectmen. Aqueduct companies may dig in highways for the placing of pipes with approval of the selectmen. Certain corporations using or transporting steam, hot water, refrigerating materials or pneumatic pressure also may dig in highways with consent of the selectmen.

Construction for water supply. A town may dig up or raise any land or highway for laying pipes and constructing a water supply. All work performed on highways, other than state highways, is subject to the direction of the selectmen.

Liability for damages. A person may recover damages for injury to his person or property resulting from a highway defect or lack of repairs in a highway which might have been prevented by reasonable diligence and care on the part of the town. The person injured is required to give notice to one of the selectmen or to the town clerk or treasurer within 30 days. If the injury is caused by snow or ice, notice is to be given within ten days. A town is not liable during construction or repairs if a highway has been closed or other means taken to caution the public against entering.

Trees in highways. Trees may be planted within the boundaries of a highway only with approval of the tree warden and in a location satisfactory to the selectmen or road commissioners. A tree is not to be removed except with the approval of the selectmen after a hearing if objection is made by one or more persons. The tree warden may remove trees which are less than one and one-half inches in diameter. He may trim or cut down trees and bushes which obstruct a highway if ordered by the selectmen, road commissioners or highway surveyor. Tree wardens may make rules and regulations which have the effect of by-laws when approved by the selectmen.

Ditches or drains. Town highway officers, county commissioners and the state Department of Public Works may construct ditches or drains for draining a highway and may take land by eminent domain if required.

Water courses. A town highway surveyor or road commissioner may have a water course relocated by the side of a highway. The selectmen may order alterations in the work on complaint of any person whose building or business is inconvenienced or obstructed.

Gravel pits. The selectmen or road commissioners may purchase or take by eminent domain any land in the town, which is not in public use or not owned by another town, for use as a gravel pit or place from which may be taken necessary materials for road construction.

Improvement associations. A town with public grounds or open spaces which are located on highways and not needed for public travel may give the care and improvement of such land to an improvement association. The association is to have the control of such property under the direction of the selectmen or road commissioners.

Sidewalks. Selectmen or road commissioners may establish sidewalks, determine the grade and specify the materials which are to be used. They also may order the rebuilding of existing sidewalks. A sidewalk is not to be dug up or constructed except with their approval.

Sidewalk assessments. In ordering construction of a new sidewalk or one of a more permanent nature, the selectmen or road commissioners may provide for special assessments on abutting property not exceeding half the cost of the sidewalk. If the town by-laws so provide, the total amount assessed on any individual property shall not exceed one per cent of its assessed valuation. Assessments are to be recorded with the registry of deeds.

Drawbridges. If a town neglects maintenance or repair of a drawbridge over navigable waters between two towns, the county commissioners may pass an order upon application of selectmen of the other town.

HOUSING AND REDEVELOPMENT

Housing authority. A town meeting may vote to provide for the organization of a housing authority whenever it determines that one is needed. Four members of the authority are appointed by the selectmen to serve only until their successors are elected at the next annual town meeting. One member is appointed by the State Housing Board.

Removal of members. Selectmen may make or receive written charges against a member of a housing authority and may remove him after a hearing. They may also suspend such member pending final action.

Selectmen may prefer charges against a member appointed by the board, and the board may remove him after a hearing.

Redevelopment project. If a housing authority decides that a redevelopment project should be started in the town, it must apply for approval to the State Housing Board. The State Housing Board is required to hold a public hearing if a written request is made within ten days by the housing authority, the selectmen or 25 taxable inhabitants of the town.

Redevelopment authority. If a town meeting determines that there is need for a redevelopment authority in the town and the housing authority, if any, gives its consent, a redevelopment authority is to be organized. The members are to be appointed in the same manner as provided for members of a housing authority.

Acquisition of prior projects. A redevelopment authority, with the consent of the selectmen and pursuant to an agreement with the housing authority, may take over a planned or an existing redevelopment project which was started by the housing authority.

Urban redevelopment corporation. An urban redevelopment corporation may be formed to carry out a redevelopment project authorized and approved by the State Housing Board. An application to the State Housing Board for the formation of such a corporation is transmitted to the selectmen of a town in which the proposed project is located. The selectmen ask the planning board, if any, to make a report on the application. The planning board, after a hearing, submits its report to the selectmen with its approval or disapproval. The selectmen then send the report of the planning board to the State Housing Board with their own approval or disapproval of the project. If the town has no planning board, the duties of a planning board relative to a hearing and report are performed by the selectmen.

Approval of application. The State Housing Board may approve the application to form the corporation if it has the approval of the selectmen and the planning board, if any, and if other requirements are met. The State Housing Board may suggest changes in the project, and if the persons seeking to form the corporation agree to the changes, they may submit an amended application. The State Housing Board may approve or disapprove the amended application, but if fundamental changes are made it must be transmitted to the selectmen of the town for action in the same manner as required for the original application.

Change in project. An urban redevelopment corporation may apply to the State Housing Board for a change in the type and character of buildings on a project. If fundamental changes are proposed, the application is transmitted to the selectmen for action similar to that required for other applications.

LICENSES

Licensing authority. The selectmen are defined as the local licensing authorities in the chapter of state laws relating to local licenses. The licensing and regulation of alcoholic beverages has been discussed under "Alcoholic Beverages."

Categories of licenses. Selectmen may license amusements, billiard tables, sippio tables, bowling alleys, cabarets, carousels, dances, dancing schools, employment offices, exhibitions, ferris wheels, inclined railways, junk dealers, lunch carts on public highways, picnic groves, roller skating rinks, shooting galleries, shows and theatrical performances. They also may issue licenses for outdoor exhibitions of fire fighting and for steamboats and other power boats on inland waters.

Other licenses. Selectmen may license pawnbrokers, if authorized by the by-laws, and may inspect the premises of pawnbrokers. They also license the sale of second hand articles other than books, prints, coins and stamps. Licenses are issued for victuallers and common innholders, and these are to be signed by a majority of the selectmen. Clubs may be licensed to dispense food and beverages. In towns accepting certain sections of the laws, licenses may be issued for coffee houses and tea houses and for the business of renting boats and bathing suits.

Soft drinks. Towns may provide by by-laws for licensing the sale of non-intoxicating beverages other than by innholders, victuallers, druggists, groceries or markets and for the sale of beverages not for consumption on the premises.

Auctioneers. Selectmen may issue a license as an auctioneer to any person who has resided in the town for six months. The fee for a one-year license is $2. They also may issue a special license to a person who is not an inhabitant of the town to be an auctioneer on certain specified days for the sale of real estate, livestock, produce or general farm equipment for a fee of $5 for each day. A special license is required for the sale of merchandise from any business which is represented to be insolvent or bankrupt.

Lodging houses. Licensing authorities may issue a license to lodging houses for five or more persons. It may be free or at a fee fixed by the selectmen not in excess of $2. The houses are subject to inspection by the selectmen, and they may require the house to keep a register which is available to the selectmen and the police.

Peddlers. The selectmen may require a license and regulate the sale by peddlers of meat, butter, cheese, fish, fresh fruits and vegetables. A license is not required for the sale of fish obtained by a person's own labor, for fruit, vegetables or farm products raised by a person or his family or sales of eggs and milk products other than frozen desserts by a person licensed to sell milk. The selectmen may regulate the sale by peddlers of newspapers, religious publications, ice, plants, uncultivated flowers, fruits, nuts and berries for which a license or fee is not required. Wholesalers, jobbers and persons selling by means of samples or catalogs are not considered as peddlers.

The state Division of Standards and Necessaries of Life may issue a license for the sale within the town by peddlers of certain goods. An applicant must present a certificate of morals and integrity signed by a majority of the selectmen. The state may also issue a license for sales in any city or town. A county license also is issued by the state for sales by peddlers in each county. The selectmen may make rules and regulations for sales by peddlers under state licenses.

Sales by minors. Selectmen may make regulations relative to bootblacks and the sale by minors of goods, wares, and merchandise which may be sold by adults without a license. They may prohibit such sales or require a minor to obtain a permit to sell such things.

Children's performances. Children under 15 years of age are not allowed to appear as participants in a theatre or other public exhibition; but the local licensing authority may give written permission for appearances in non-commercial exhibitions or for limited commercial appearances with approval of the state Commissioner of Labor and Industries. Selectmen may give special written permission for children to take part in any festival, concert or musical exhibition.

Bicycle registration. The selectmen of towns not having a police department which accept a pertinent section of law may register the bicycles of residents.

Busses. The selectmen are to issue licenses for the carrying of passengers for hire by motor vehicles in the manner of a railway company or between fixed points. They may limit the number of vehicles except on highways under the Metropolitan District Commission. This does not apply to interstate vehicles or to trolley motor or trackless trolley transportation. The MDC and the Massachusetts Turnpike Authority shall be the licensing authority for motor carriers using their highways.

Sale of firearms. Selectmen or chiefs of police in a town may grant licenses for the sale or rental of firearms and may specify the location of the business. The licensing authority to whom application is made shall require fingerprints of the applicant and shall forward one copy to the

Commissioner of Public Safety. Licenses are to be recorded in books or forms kept for that purpose, and the licensee is to be provided with a sales record book by the Commissioner.

Suspension or revocation of license. Licensing authorities may forfeit an individual's license upon receiving satisfactory proof that conditions of issuance have been violated. At the same time they must notify the Commissioner of Public Safety of such forfeiture.

Carrying of firearms. The selectmen or persons authorized by them may issue permits to carry firearms within the state or to possess a machine gun. They also may grant a license to purchase or rent a pistol or revolver. Fingerprints of an applicant for a permit shall be forwarded by the licensing authority to the Commissioner of Public Safety.

Pinball machines. Selectmen may grant licenses to keep automatic amusement devices, or pinball machines, as approved by the state director of Standards and Necessaries of Life.

Second hand automobiles. Licenses are issued by the selectmen for the sale of second hand automobiles. These are of three classes. Class 1 is for new car dealers whose used car business is incidental to their regular business. Class 2 is for used car dealers whose principal business is the buying and selling of used cars. Class 3 licenses are for motor vehicle junk dealers and those who deal in second hand parts. These can be issued only after a hearing with seven days notice to abutting property owners. The selectmen may investigate all classes of applicants to determine that they are proper persons to engage in the business. The premises of licensed dealers are subject to inspection by the selectmen and the chief of police.

Trailer camps. Trailer parking lots and overnight cabins are licensed by the board of health.

Tag days. Selectmen may grant special licenses to charitable organizations and veterans' posts for the sale of flags, badges, medals, buttons, flowers, souvenirs and other small articles on a particular day under such conditions as the selectmen think proper. No sales can be made by persons under 16 years of age.

Parking lots. In towns accepting a particular section of law, the selectmen may license open air parking spaces with approval of the head of the fire department.

Stable licenses. Selectmen of towns with a population of 5,000 or less may issue stable licenses for the keeping of more than four horses in specified buildings or places.

Vehicle regulations. The town by-laws or rules and orders of the selectmen may provide for the regulation of carriages and vehicles, and they may require a license fee of $1.

Furnaces and steam engines. Selectmen may license furnaces for melting iron or making glass, also stationary steam engines for saw mills using fuel other than coal, after a hearing held at the expense of the applicant with 14 days notice.

Boxing matches. Boxing matches under a license of the State Boxing Commission are permitted in a town if the pertinent sections of law are accepted by the voters at the annual meeting or a special town meeting called by the selectmen. The question of acceptance is to be submitted on petition of ten per cent of the total voters filed with the town clerk at least 30 days before the meeting. After acceptance, the question again may be submitted on petition of ten per cent of the voters filed with the town clerk 30 days before a meeting, and acceptance may be rescinded if so voted by the town.

Sunday amateur sports. Amateur sports also may be licensed on Sunday by the selectmen or by officials in charge of a park or playground subject to regulation by the selectmen.

Sunday amusement parks. Selectmen may license various enterprises on Sunday at amusement parks or beach resorts on prescribed terms and conditions. These include bowling alleys, shooting galleries, photographic studios, games and amusement devices.

Sunday bowling alleys. In towns accepting a section of law, the selectmen may issue Sunday licenses for bowling alleys.

Sunday entertainments. The selectmen upon receiving a written application may grant a Sunday license to hold a public entertainment on such terms and conditions as they may prescribe. Such an event may include musical entertainment furnished by mechanical or electrical means and is subject to the provisions of law relating to performances by children under 15 years of age. The use of motion pictures, radio or television is not a ground for refusal of a Sunday license.

Sunday games. By the acceptance of other sections, outdoor sports or games and indoor basketball games may be held on Sunday, with licenses issued by the selectmen unless the games are held in a park or playground. In the latter case the officials in charge of the grounds are the licensing authority. All Sunday sports and games are subject to regulation by the selectmen.

Sunday soda and beverages. In towns accepting another section of law, selectmen may issue Sunday licenses to retail dealers in frozen desserts, ice cream mix, confectionery, soda or fruit who do not sell alcoholic beverages.

Sunday work or labor. The chief of police or chairman of selectmen may issue a one day permit for Sunday work or labor upon such terms and conditions as he deems reasonable. Such a permit may be issued not more than six days in advance.

LOW LANDS AND SWAMPS

Improvement of low land areas. The state or any city or town owning meadow, swamp, marsh, beach or other low lands may be a party to proceedings for the improvement of low land areas to the same extent as individual proprietors. The purposes of such improvement are to drain land, to remove obstructions in rivers and streams, to eradicate mosquitoes in infested areas, to drain land for agriculture or industrial uses and to protect the public health.

Action by selectmen. Individuals and corporations qualifying as proprietors may join in a petition to the State Reclamation Board stating their desire to improve the area. Action is to be taken by the selectmen. Notice of a hearing is given by the state board to the selectmen, other petitioners and all known proprietors of the lands affected. The board decides if organization of a reclamation district is necessary.

Access to lands by owners. Any town or person owning low land, ponds, swamps, quarries, mines or mineral deposits which cannot be approached, drained or used because of a highway or lands belonging to others may construct roads, drains, ditches, tunnels or railways to such land and take the land of other persons if required by public convenience or necessity.

Petition by land owner. A person desiring to provide access to his land by making such improvements is required to file a petition with the county commissioners of the county where the greater part of the land lies. If the land is entirely in one town, the petition is made to the selectmen and filed with the town clerk. Selectmen are to receive $2 for each day of service on such a petition.

Proceedings by selectmen. Following notice and hearing and after an inspection, the selectmen may lay out and establish the improvements for access to such land and may take property by eminent domain. They are to assess the amount awarded as damages upon the persons for whose use the improvements are made in proportion to the benefit received by each.

Petition to county commissioners. A person aggrieved by refusal of selectmen to make an order on such a petition may make a petition within one year to the county commissioners, who proceed in the same manner as though the petition originally had been filed with them.

MILITIA

Request for aid of militia. The selectmen may request the Governor to order the militia to aid civil authorities in case of riot. In the event of a catastrophe or disaster, they may issue a precept directed to the commander of militia in their county requesting such assistance. The town is liable for the expenses of the militia in rendering assistance.

Rental of armory by state. The selectmen of a town having an armory, air installation or other military facilities which are rented to the state are required to submit an annual bill for rental to the state quartermaster, who notifies the selectmen of the sum allowed.

Purchase of armory by state. The state may purchase an armory or other facilities from a town, with approval of the Governor and Council. The value of the land and buildings is determined by agreement between the selectmen and the state Armory Commission.

Unorganized militia. The law also gives to the selectmen responsibility for assembling and drafting the unorganized militia upon proclamation of the Governor in case of war, invasion or riot. The unorganized militia consists of all able-bodied male residents between 17 and 45 years of age.

MUNICIPAL LIGHTING

Municipal light board. Towns owning a gas or electric plant may elect a municipal light board of three members for three year overlapping terms.

Manager of municipal lighting. The municipal light board appoints a manager of municipal lighting. The manager has charge of the operation and management of the plant under the direction and control of the board. His compensation and term of office is fixed by the board and he is required to give a bond approved by them. In towns without a municipal light board, the selectmen appoint a manager of municipal lighting. In all towns, accounts of the municipal lighting plant are subject to inspection by the selectmen and they approve all bills and payrolls.

Estimates of lighting plant. The manager of municipal lighting is to furnish estimates of income and expenses for the ensuing year to the municipal light board or to the selectmen in towns not having such a board.

Reports to state department. The manager of municipal lighting, selectmen or municipal light board, if any, are to submit the books and accounts of the municipal lighting plant to the state Department of Public Utilities and are to furnish any statement or information required by it. The selectmen or municipal light board, if any, are to make an annual report to the state department for the preceding fiscal year. The report is to be signed by a majority of the selectmen or board and by the manager of municipal lighting.

Electricity from street railway. A street railway company may manufacture electricity incident to its operations. The selectmen may grant it authority to erect and maintain poles, wires and other devices on highways and bridges.

Contract with street railway. A town may contract for the purchase of electricity from a street railway company for the use of the municipality or its inhabitants.

Fixing of contract price. If a town votes to purchase electricity from a street railway company and is unable to agree upon the price at the time of expiration of a contract, the selectmen may apply to the state Department of Public Utilities and the department may fix the price after a hearing.

Exemption from standards for gas. On application of the selectmen of a town with a municipal lighting plant, the state Department of Public Utilities may exempt the plant from the requirement of furnishing gas of the established standard if local conditions warrant such action.

Training and employment of cadet engineers in municipal light and gas plants. A town owning or operating a municipal light plant or gas plant may train and employ cadet engineers by contract, under which cadets may pursue engineering courses at a college or university while taking on-the-job training at the plant.

The municipal light board or in towns having no board, the selectmen, shall negotiate contracts and supervise cadet training.

Applications for appointment as cadet engineer. The municipal light board shall appoint a selection committee of five to seven members, including the municipal lighting manager and two educators resident in town. They shall serve at no compensation for one year terms.

NUISANCES

Abatement of nuisances. Selectmen have the same power to abate and remove nuisances as is given to boards of health under the chapter of state laws relating to public health.

Petition for abatement. A person injured by a public health nuisance may petition the board of health for abatement. The board sets the time and place for a hearing and gives notice to the persons concerned and to the chairman of the selectmen, except in towns where the selectmen constitute the board of health. The notice is required to be in writing and served by a person authorized to serve civil process. The board of health must give notice of its decision to the assessors and the parties to whom notice of the hearing is required to be given.

Dangerous buildings. In towns accepting certain sections of the statutes, the selectmen may declare a burned, dilapidated or dangerous building to be a nuisance. They may prescribe its alteration or disposition after a hearing and written notice to the owner.

Lack of fireproof construction. A building not erected in conformity with regulations requiring fireproof construction may be removed as a nuisance by the selectmen. This is discussed under the heading "Building Inspection."

Smoke nuisance. The emission of dense smoke may be declared a nuisance under certain conditions in towns accepting pertinent provisions of law, unless it results from operations under a smoke permit signed by a majority of the selectmen and the town clerk. The selectmen may designate persons each year to enforce smoke regulations.

Unlawful use of temporary structure. If complaint is made to the selectmen that a booth, shed or other temporary structure is used for gambling or the sale of liquor within one mile of a place of public gathering, they may close the place, declare it to be a public nuisance and cause the building to be destroyed.

Insect pest control. Gypsy and brown tail moths and other insect pests are by law public nuisances. A local superintendent of insect pest control is to be appointed by the town manager, if any, or by the selectmen. The state Commissioner of Natural Resources is to be notified of the appointment. In case of a vacancy or in the absence of the local superintendent, the manager or selectmen designate a person to perform the duties.

The financial liability of each town is determined annually by the Commissioner who notifies the manager or selectmen.

PLANNING AND CONSERVATION

Planning board. Towns of more than 10,000 population are required to establish a planning board consisting of from five to nine members who serve for five year overlapping terms. The planning board is to make studies and prepare plans of the resources, possibilities and needs of the town. It is to submit a report and recommendations to the selectmen and an annual report to the town meeting.

Planning board in small towns. Towns under 10,000 population may establish a planning board and may authorize the selectmen to act as such until one is created.

Official map. The town may adopt an official map prepared under the direction of the planning board. If the subdivision control law is not in effect in a town adopting an official map, the town shall provide for a board of appeals.

Change in official map. Any change in or an addition to the official map by a town meeting is not effective until a public hearing has been held by the selectmen after ten days notice.

Selectmen as board of appeals. Pending the creation of a board of appeals under the subdivision control law, the selectmen are to act as a board of appeals. The board is to consist of at least three members appointed by the selectmen for overlapping terms so arranged that one shall expire each year. The town by-laws may provide for the appointment of associate members to serve in the absence of regular members.

Selectmen as board of survey. In towns which accepted the provisions of law before 1936, the selectmen constitute a board of survey until it is terminated under the planning law of 1953.

Selectmen as park commissioners. In towns which have not elected a board of park commissioners or which have not authorized the town planning board to act as a board of park commissioners, the selectmen are to act as such a board.

Powers of selectmen. Provisions of the planning laws are not to abridge the powers of the selectmen in any manner except as specifically provided in those sections of the laws. The subdivision control law is not to abridge the powers of the selectmen or other officers in regard to highways except as specifically provided.

Industrial development. A town may vote to create a development and industrial commission for the promotion and development of its industrial resources. It is to be composed of from five to 15 members with five year overlapping terms. The appointments are made by the manager in manager towns and by the selectmen in other towns.

Conservation commissions. Towns may establish a conservation commission for the promotion and development of natural resources and for protection of watershed resources of the town.

This commission may recommend conservation programs to the selectmen. With the selectmen's approval it may recommend programs for the local area to the Department of Natural Resources. Commission members are appointed by the selectmen, but in towns having a town manager they shall be appointed by him with approval of the selectmen.

Commissions, with approval of the selectmen, may receive gifts of funds, lands, buildings and other properties in the name of the town.

Eminent domain for conservation purposes. Use of eminent domain powers to acquire land for conservation and recreation purposes is subject to approval of the Board of Natural Resources, the Governor and Council, and the board of selectmen in town(s) concerned.

Selectmen must approve within 30 days the taking of land within their town by the Commissioner of Natural Resources for conservation and recreation purposes under eminent domain authority. Failure to act within this time constitutes tacit approval.

PLAYGROUNDS AND RECREATION

Referendum on playgrounds. In towns of more than 5,000 population the question of providing playgrounds may be submitted to the voters by petition of at least ten per cent of the voters filed with the selectmen 15 days before the annual town meeting.

Recreation centers. A town may acquire land and buildings for a public playground or recreation center and conduct recreation activities for which admission may be charged. Such an activity is managed in any of four ways, as the town meeting may decide:

(a) by the board of park commissioners, school committee or planning board.
(b) by a playground or recreation commission, appointed by the selectmen or moderator or elected by the voters at a town meeting.
(c) distributed among a board of park commissioners, school committee, planning board and such a playground or recreation commission, or any two or more of them.
(d) by a committee consisting of one member each designated by any or all of such boards or commissions, together with two or more members at large appointed by the selectmen or moderator or elected by the voters.

Playgrounds in tenement districts. In towns located in the metropolitan parks district, owners of tenement buildings which adjoin open spaces may apply to the park commissioners, or the Metropolitan District Commission if the town has no park commissioners, to lease such open spaces for neighborhood playgrounds with approval of the town board of health. The land may be leased for not over 15 years for a rental not more than the amount of the taxes and is subject to renewal. The owners of the tenement buildings are to have the care and control of the land under the supervision of the park commissioners or the selectmen of a town not having park commissioners.

Gymnasium and swimming pool. Towns are authorized to appropriate money to establish and maintain a swimming pool or public gymnasium, to be managed under the direction of the selectmen.

Use of facilities by town. Land and buildings acquired for recreation purposes also may be used for town meetings or by any town department with the consent of the town officer or board having charge of the land or building. This applies to property acquired for playground or recreation purposes, but not to property acquired solely for park purposes.

Coasting on highways. Selectmen may designate parts of highways for coasting, other than on state highways, and may regulate the use of vehicles in such places during certain hours.

POLICE

Police department under selectmen. A town may have a police department under the direction of the selectmen by accepting the pertinent section of the statutes. The selectmen appoint the chief of police and other officers and make rules and regulations for the department. The chief has control of police officers and town property used by the department. In towns not under civil service, the selectmen may remove the chief and other officers at pleasure.

Authority of chief. By accepting a different section of the laws, the chief has authority to make rules and regulations subject to the approval of the selectmen. The rules are effective in 30 days if the selectmen fail to act. The selectmen may remove the chief and other officers only for cause and after a hearing.

Commissioner of public safety. A town may vote to have a commissioner of public safety. The selectmen appoint the commissioner, who is chief of the police and fire departments. The commissioner appoints a deputy as police chief and one or more deputy fire chiefs, subject to approval of the selectmen. The commissioner also fixes the compensation of policemen and firemen with the approval of the selectmen.

Reserve force. Towns with an organized police department which accept a section of the laws may establish a reserve force. The reserve force is appointed in the same manner as regular police officers. Its members are subject to rules and regulations of the selectmen and may be removed by them. In towns under civil service, the reserve force is subject to the requirements of civil service.

Police services in other towns. At the request of the mayor, selectmen or chief of police of another municipality, the selectmen may provide police officers for service in the other city or town. Their compensation and travelling expenses are paid by the city or town making the request.

Police services on federal reservations. Selectmen may provide police officers for duty on a federal government reservation in the town or adjoining the town, upon requisition of the commanding officer or person in charge of the reservation.

Working days for police duty. In towns accepting one of several optional sections of the laws, members of the police department are to have one day off for a varying number of days of service, depending upon the specific provision adopted.

Police weapons. Police officers are to carry such weapons when on duty as determined by the town manager of a manager town or by the selectmen of other towns.

Offering of reward. Selectmen may offer a suitable reward of not more than $500 in any one case, to be paid by the town for the apprehension of a person who has committed a felony.

Loans on personal property. Loans on collateral security, such as household and personal goods, are required to be entered by the lender in a record book which is open to the inspection of the selectmen and the chief of police.

Dispersal of riot. If 12 or more persons armed with clubs or weapons, or 30 or more persons whether armed or not, are riotously or tumultuously assembled, each of the selectmen, justices of the peace, county sheriff and deputies is required to go among them and command them to disperse. A penalty is provided for any selectmen who neglects or refuses to suppress a riot.

Motor vehicles. Selectmen may make special regulations relating to the speed of motor vehicles on particular highways with approval of the state Department of Public Works and Registrar of Motor Vehicles. They may regulate the use of vehicles and prohibit vehicles on certain roads with approval of the Department of Public Works. Vehicles are not to be excluded from state highways or from local highways leading to another town. Selectmen also may regulate the speed and use of vehicles on private ways and parking areas upon written application of the owners or of the person having control of the area with consent of the owner. Regulations applying to private land are effective only one year at a time. Special constables for enforcing motor vehicle laws when wearing a uniform and badge may be appointed by the selectmen. The chairman of the selectmen in towns not having a police department is to notify the Registrar of Motor Vehicles of certain accidents.

PUBLIC WORKS

Board of public works. A town may establish a board of public works by accepting the sections of law authorizing such action. The board is to consist of three members elected by the town meeting for three year overlapping terms.

Creation of board. The question of establishing a board of public works is to be submitted to an annual town meeting by vote of a town meeting called for the purpose at least 90 days before the annual meeting. If the earlier meeting fails to approve submission of the question, it may be submitted upon petition of ten per cent of the voters filed with the selectmen at least 60 days before the annual meeting. A town may vote to revoke acceptance of the permissive law after the expiration of three years.

Powers of board. A board of public works has all the powers and duties conferred and imposed upon road commissioners, surveyors of highways and superintendents of streets, and those of water and sewer commissioners, park and cemetery commissioners and a municipal light board. It also takes over the functions of a forestry department, tree warden and moth superintendent. The town may provide by by-law for the board to assume any other duties which reasonably are related to a board of public works. These may include providing of engineering services, garbage and rubbish collection and maintenance and repair of town buildings and property.

Superintendent of public works. The board appoints a superintendent of public works, who performs the duties transferred to the board under the supervision and direction of the board.

Status of board. A board of public works is the lawful successor of all town boards, departments and officers whose functions it assumes. In towns where such a board is in existence, references in the laws and in this handbook to former boards and officers should be construed to refer to the board of public works or superintendent of public works, as the case may be.

Selectmen as public works board. By a special town meeting vote or by petition of ten per cent of the voters at least 60 days before an annual meeting, a town may at its annual meeting vote to have the selectmen act as a board of public works.

SCHOOLS

Eyeglasses and hearing aids for school children. The selectmen are to supervise the spending of any appropriation for the purchase of eyeglasses and hearing aids for school children whose parents are unable to furnish them.

Regional school operating funds. Between January 1st and the date of annual town appropriations, the treasurer of any member town may, with approval of the selectmen, make payments to the regional school district not to exceed in total one third of the amount apportioned.

School appropriation deficiency. If a town does not appropriate sufficient money for schools, the Superior Court on petition of ten taxable inhabitants may determine the amount of the deficiency and order the selectmen, treasurer and assessors to provide the necessary amount, together with a sum equal to 25 per cent of such amount. If this is ordered after the annual tax rate has been fixed, the town treasurer is to borrow the money with approval of the selectmen.

School services. The school committee, with approval of the selectmen, may establish extended school services for children from three to 14 years of age whose mothers are employed. This requires further approval by the state Commissioner of Education. If the town has a contract with the federal government for extended school services, the town treasurer, with approval of the selectmen, may borrow outside the debt limit in anticipation of the federal grant.

SEWERS

Sewer installations. A town may adopt a sewer system for the whole town or part of the town. Selectmen, road commissioners or sewer commissioners may install a main drain or common sewer wherever they deem necessary and may take land by eminent domain for such a purpose. They may prescribe the manner in which it is to be built and the materials which are to be used.

Sewage disposal. A town may purchase or take land by eminent domain for a sewage disposal plant, with approval of the state Department of Public Works after a hearing.

Sewer assessments. A town may provide special assessments for sewers upon the owners of land at a fixed and uniform rate. The selectmen, road commissioners or sewer commissioners may extend the time for payment of sewer assessments on land which is not built upon, but interest at 4 per cent is to be paid from the time the assessment was made. Assessments for particular sewers are set by the selectmen, road commissioners or sewer commissioners. They also have authority to determine that a person should pay for the permanent privilege of sewers instead of paying an assessment.

Sewer use charges. The selectmen, road commissioners or sewer commissioners may establish just and equitable charges for the use of sewers.

Regulations. The selectmen, road commissioners or sewer commissioners may make necessary regulations relating to the use of sewers and may impose penalties.

TOWN MEETINGS

Calling town meetings. Town meetings are called by warrant issued by the selectmen. The annual town meeting is required to be held in February, March or April. Special meetings may be held at such times as the selectmen may order. Selectmen are required to call a special meeting within 45 days at the request of 200 voters or 20 per cent of the total voters, whichever is the lesser number. For some specific purposes, special meetings must be called by petition of a definite number of voters specified in the particular statute.

Warrant for meeting. The warrant must be issued at least seven days before the meeting and be directed to constables or other persons to give notice as provided in the town by-laws, or in a manner approved by the Attorney General if there are no by-laws.

Subjects included in warrant. The warrant must include all subjects to be acted on at the meeting. The selectmen are required to include for the annual meeting all subjects requested in writing by ten or more voters. For a special town meeting, they must include any subjects requested by 100 voters or 10 per cent of the total voters, whichever is the lesser number.

Meetings in more than one place. A town meeting may be held in more than one place provided the places are connected by a public address system with loudspeakers so that all may hear and be heard if they wish to speak.

If the meeting becomes so crowded that voters are excluded or cannot hear or be heard, the moderator may consult with the selectmen then present and adjourn to another date not later than 14 days afterwards when adequate facilities will be available.

Call other than by selectmen. If there should be no selectmen in office, the town clerk may call a town meeting. If the selectmen unreasonably refuse to call a meeting, a justice of the peace may issue a warrant for the meeting on application of 100 voters or 10 per cent of the total voters.

Acting moderator. In the event that the town clerk is absent at a town meeting or if there is no town clerk, the chairman of the selectmen presides in the absence of the moderator until a moderator or assistant moderator is elected.

Revocation of special acts. A town meeting may revoke the acceptance of a special act after a period of three years. The question is submitted by the selectmen on petition of 10 per cent of the voters filed not less than 90 days before the annual town meeting. The right of revocation does not apply to towns of more than 15,000 population and is not applicable to laws on civil service, retirement systems, authority for capital outlay, authority for a public improvement or to membership in a district with other towns.

Representative town meeting (RTM). Any town in which a representative town meeting has been established may adopt the standard form of representative town meeting on petition of five per cent of the registered voters filed with the selectmen not less than 90 days before the annual town meeting. The selectmen direct the town clerk to place the question on the official ballot.

RTM Precincts. Upon its adoption, the selectmen are required to divide the territory of the town into voting precincts containing not less than 400 voters. The boundaries are to be reviewed by the selectmen and revised if need be in December of every fifth year. Boundaries are to be reviewed and revised in December of any year if so directed by a vote of the representative town meeting held not later than November 20.

RTM Change in precincts. The selectmen are to file a report with the town clerk, registrars of voters and assessors within ten days after establishing or revising the voting precincts. They also are to file a map or description of the precincts and the names of the registered voters in each. These are posted in the town hall and in a public place in every precinct.

RTM Referendum on actions. A petition of 3 per cent of the voters for a referendum on certain actions of the representative town meeting which are specified in the statutes may be filed with the selectmen within five days of a special meeting. The selectmen are to call a special meeting of the voters of the town for submission of the questions contained in the petition. An action of the representative town meeting cannot be reversed by the voters of a town unless 20 per cent of the total registered voters so vote at a special meeting.

TOWN OFFICERS AND EMPLOYEES

Election of town officers. Certain town officers are required by law to be elected by vote of the town. The selectmen must be elected, but the town may provide by by-law that the selectmen appoint any of the other officers mentioned, namely:

Assessors and assistant assessors, auditors, board of health, board of public welfare, town clerk, collector of taxes, constables, highway surveyors, road commissioners, school committee, sewer commissioners, treasurer and tree warden.

Selectmen acting as certain officers. By vote of a town meeting held 60 days before the annual meeting or on petition of 10 per cent of the voters filed with the selectmen at least 60 days before the annual meeting, the meeting is to vote upon the question of having the selectmen act as or perform the duties of any of the following officers:

Assessors, board of health, board of public welfare, board of public works, municipal light board, park commissioners, public safety commission, sewer commissioners, water commissioners, water and light commissioners and water and sewer board.

Term of selectmen. If a town which elects its selectmen for one year votes to have them act as or perform the duties of other town officers, the selectmen thereafter shall be elected for three year overlapping terms.

Appointment of town officers. By means of a vote or petition similar to that authorizing selectmen to act as other officers, the annual town meeting may vote upon the question of having any of the following officers appointed by the selectmen:

Assessors, cemetery commissioners, chief of fire department, chief of police department, superintendent of streets and tree warden.

Repeal of authorization. After the expiration of three years a town may vote, at a meeting held 30 days before the annual meeting, to rescind the authority for the selectmen to act as such officers or to make such appointments.

Assessors. Towns are required to elect one, three or five assessors for a term of three years unless the town votes that assessors be appointed by the selectmen. The authority for a single assessor was added by an amendment in 1953. If a town votes to have the selectmen appoint assessors, they are required to appoint three or five if the town has accepted a particular section of the laws.

Selectmen as assessors. The selectmen serve as assessors in towns which have not authorized the election of such officers. In such cases, selectmen are required to take an additional oath of office as assessors. If the assessors or selectmen acting as assessors fail to perform their duties, the state Commissioner of Corporations and Taxation may appoint three or more persons as assessors for the town.

Counsel for assessors. The assessors or selectmen acting as assessors in towns not having a town counsel may employ legal counsel in certain cases at the expense of the town.

Constables. Towns are required by statute to elect one or more constables for a term of one or three years unless the town votes that they be appointed. Another section of the law authorizes the selectmen in any town to appoint as many constables as they deem necessary for terms not exceeding one year.

Applications for constable. Applicants for appointment as constable make written application to the selectmen with such information as the selectmen may require. Selectmen are required to investigate the reputation and character of the applicants and may request the chief of police to assist in the investigation.

Police officers. The selectmen may appoint police officers to hold office at the pleasure of the selectmen.

Purchasing agent. Towns accepting a particular section of the laws may establish a purchasing department, consisting of a purchasing agent and such assistants as the selectmen determine. The purchasing agent and assistants are appointed by the selectmen.

Town accountant. A town may authorize the selectmen to appoint a town accountant to exercise and perform the powers and duties of town auditor, and the town may abolish the position of town auditor.

Veterans' services director. Towns which are not in a district for veterans' services are to have a department of veterans' services under a director appointed by the selectmen. It is the duty of such an officer to furnish information, advice and assistance to veterans. There also is to be an unpaid advisory board of from five to 15 members appointed by the selectmen.

Water or sewer superintendent. If a town votes to have the selectmen act as water or sewer commissioners, they may appoint a superintendent of the water or sewer department or designate the superintendent of streets to act in that capacity.

Weighers and measurers. The selectmen are to appoint weighers and measurers of certain commodities for a term of one year upon the written request of any person buying, selling or transporting such goods or commodities. The weighers need not be residents of the town and at least one of them shall not be in a business concerned with the commodity to be weighed.

Weighers of fish. The selectmen in towns where salt water fish are landed from vessels are to appoint public weighers of fish for one year, who may appoint deputy weighers with approval of the chairman of the selectmen. The weigher and deputy weighers are not to be in the fish business.

Custodian of state reports. The selectmen are authorized to designate a person to have charge of books, reports and laws received from the state, or may place such publications in the public library. The town clerk is responsible for them unless someone else is designated.

Tenure of town clerk. A town may accept a provision of law permitting a town clerk with five years service to hold office during good behavior. In this event, the town clerk can be removed only for cause after a hearing for reasons given in writing by the selectmen.

Advance on travel expenses. With approval of the selectmen, advances may be made to any officer or employee in anticipation of necessary travel expenses.

Suggestion awards. The chairman of the selectmen appoints a committee to judge suggestions of town employees for improving municipal services when cash awards are to be given for suggestions.

Employees' work week. In towns accepting a section of the statutes the services of town employees are restricted to five days and 40 hours in any one week, except in an emergency determined by the selectmen or an official designated by them. Additional service may be authorized and paid as overtime. This does not apply to policemen, firemen, school teachers, offices established by law or groups specifically exempted.

Half holiday permitted. The selectmen may grant employees a half holiday in each week on written recommendation of any department head during such part of the year as the selectmen determine. This does not apply to towns which have accepted a section of law providing for a 40 hour week.

Indemnification of employees. By adopting a section of law, a town may indemnify town officers and employees for the defense of any claim arising from the operation of motor vehicles or vessels. The selectmen are to ascertain that the person was on official duty and the defense or settlement is to be conducted by the town counsel or an attorney employed by the selectmen in towns not having a town counsel. It does not apply to towns where such claims are covered by insurance.

Indemnification of policemen and firemen. Another section of law which may be accepted by a town permits the indemnification of retired policemen and firemen or next of kin for medical or hospital expenses connected with a disability for which they were retired. Approval is required by the majority of a panel consisting of the chairman of the retirement board, the town counsel and a physician appointed by the manager of a town having a town manager or the selectmen of other towns.

Group insurance. Towns accepting a chapter of law may provide employees with group life, accident, hospital, medical and surgical insurance. The expense of premiums is equally divided between the employee and the town. Upon acceptance of the legislative act the selectmen are to execute agreements and contracts for such policies, subject to available appropriations. In towns of less than 10,000 population, employees are entitled to be included in any county insurance plan of the county in which the town is situated.

Retirement board. In towns having a contributory retirement system under the state retirement law, the system is managed by a retirement board of three members. One is the auditor, accountant or similar officer. Another is elected by members of the retirement system from among their own number. The third member is appointed by the selectmen for a three year term. The employee member of the board is chosen in such a manner as the selectmen determine for a term not exceeding three years. Town employees in towns of less than 10,000 population which accept the state retirement law are members of the county retirement system of the county in which the town is located.

Employment of veterans. In towns not under civil service, the selectmen are directed by law to take any necessary action to secure the employment of veterans in the labor service of the town in preference to all other persons. Town employees who are veterans may be given permission by the selectmen to attend the funeral of any veteran or member of the armed forces without loss of pay.

TOWN PROPERTY

Taking of land. The selectmen may purchase or take by eminent domain any land, easement or right for any municipal purpose not otherwise authorized by statute if an appropriation has been made by a two-thirds vote of the town.

Conveyance of land. Selectmen also may approve the conveyance of any land or the abandonment of any easement or right acquired other than by purchase if the town officer having charge of the land notifies the selectmen that it no longer is needed for public purposes. A two-thirds vote of the town is also needed.

Selectmen must sell land for the minimum amount specified and agreement must be recorded within six months. Actual transfer must be made within three months after the six month period.

Use of land. The town, by a two-thirds vote of the town meeting, may transfer control of any town land, including playground land but excluding park land, to a different town officer for some other town purpose if the town officer having charge of the land notifies the selectmen that it no longer is needed for its original use.

Control of property. The selectmen have control of all town property which has not been placed in the care of any particular board, officer or department by the by-laws or by vote of the town meeting. This does not apply to town property which may be rented or leased for use of veterans' posts. Selectmen are authorized to make orders for the use or disposal of town property.

Lease of property. Selectmen may lease town buildings for not over five years on such terms as they determine, except school buildings which are in actual use. They also may dispose of real and personal property of the town. They are required to hold property in trust for the schools and the promotion of education. They also are to hold and manage gifts or bequests for war memorials or public reading rooms.

Art commission. A town may vote at the annual town meeting to accept provisions of law authorizing the establishment of an art commission. Within 60 days after acceptance the school committee, public library trustees and board of park commissioners, or three similar boards designated by the town at the time of acceptance, are each to send to the selectmen the names of two citizens as nominees. The selectmen then appoint from the list of nominations an unpaid art commission of three members to serve for three year terms. The members may be removed and acceptance of the law revoked by a two-thirds vote of an annual town meeting.

Approval of buildings and ornaments. In towns having an art commission, a municipal structure is not to be erected or an ornament or work of art placed or relocated on public lands or in public buildings unless approved in writing by the commission or unless it fails to approve within 30 days. This requirement does not apply to cemeteries, drinking fountains, watering troughs or structures of public utility corporations.

Public domain. If a town decides by a two-thirds vote at the annual town meeting to acquire land as public domain for the cultivation of forest trees or for protection of the water supply, the selectmen are to issue an order within ten days for the taking of such land by eminent domain. Public domain owned by a town which is used as a forest and not as a part of water supply lands is to be in charge of a special unpaid town forest commission consisting of three members appointed by the selectmen.

VACANCIES IN OFFICE

Vacancies filled by selectmen. Vacancies in the office of selectmen are filled by election. If there is a vacancy in any other town office, except selectmen, auditor, clerk, collector or treasurer, the selectmen are to fill the vacancy in writing.

Vacancies in boards. If there is a vacancy in any board, the remaining members are to give written notice to the selectmen. After a notice of one week the selectmen together with the remaining members of the board are to fill the vacancy by ballot. A majority of all the officers entitled to vote is required.

Other offices. Vacancies in offices which are authorized by vote of the town to be filled by the selectmen are filled in the manner of the original appointment.

Finance officers. In case of a vacancy in the office of accountant, auditor, collector or treasurer, the selectmen may make a temporary appointment to be filed with the town clerk. They also may appoint a temporary highway surveyor, road commissioner or tree warden.

Auditor. If the place of one auditor is vacant, the remaining auditors may perform the duties and appoint a person to assist them. If there is no remaining auditor, one is to be appointed temporarily by the selectmen.

Trust fund commissioners. Vacancies in a board of commissioners of trust funds, which is elected by the town, are filled by the selectmen.

Town clerk. If there is a vacancy in the office of town clerk at the time of a town meeting, or if the town clerk is absent, the town meeting is to elect a temporary clerk by ballot. The votes are counted by the selectmen, if present, otherwise by three persons chosen at the meeting. For the performances of the duties of town clerk, other than those performed at the town meeting, the selectmen may fill the vacancy by appointing a town clerk in writing.

Certificate of appointment. Upon the appointment of an acting town clerk, the chairman of the selectmen is to file a proper certificate with the Secretary of the Commonwealth.

WATER SUPPLY

Board of water commissioners. Towns establishing a water supply system may create a board of water commissioners of three members or they may authorize the selectmen to act as a board of water commissioners. If a separate board is created, the town may authorize the selectmen to act as such a board temporarily until a board is elected by the town meeting.

Powers and duties. The water commissioners, or selectmen acting as such, have control of all land, property and water rights taken for water supply purposes. They are to locate hydrants, regulate the use of water, fix rates and collect water bills.

Sources of water supply. A town may purchase the right to take water from pipes and sources of supply of any municipal or other corporation. It may purchase water rights, franchises and privileges to provide its own water supply by action of the selectmen approved by a town meeting at which the voting list is used.

Taking of land for watershed purposes. The water commissioners or selectmen acting as such may take the waters of any pond or stream for a water supply by purchase or eminent domain, with approval of the state Department of Public Health.

Taking of water rights. The selectmen or water commissioners in towns not using the metropolitan water supply may take the right to draw water from any stream, pond, reservoir or ground sources by eminent domain in order to relieve an emergency if authorized by vote of the town meeting and approved by the state Department of Public Health.

Purchase of water. The water commissioners or selectmen acting as such may purchase water for a period of six months in any year from any water supply district, state or county institution or the Metropolitan District Commission.

Permits authorized by state department. The state Department of Public Health may make examinations of inland waters and streams used as sources of water supply and may issue rules and regulations to prevent pollution. The state department may delegate to the selectmen or to the board of health or water board in a town the right to grant any permit required by its rules, subject to recommendations and direction of the department.

Special assessments. Towns accepting certain sections of the statutes may adopt by-laws providing for the levy of special assessments to defray the cost of laying water pipes upon the land receiving such benefits.

Pollution of water supply. The state Department of Public Health is required to hold a hearing and take action on a petition of the selectmen stating that waters used as a source of water supply are polluted.

Enforcement by courts. The Supreme Judicial Court or Superior Court, on application by the selectmen, may enjoin a violation of law relating to pollution of a water supply.

Pipes to another town. Selectmen may designate the highways in which pipes may be laid for the water supply of another town.

WELFARE

Selectmen as welfare board. The selectmen may serve as the board of public welfare in towns where such a board is not elected. Towns which elect a board of public welfare for one year may vote that the selectmen act as such a board. If official ballots are used, the vote is to be taken at least 30 days before the annual meeting. The town may rescind such a vote in the same manner.

Public welfare agent. If the selectmen are authorized to act as a board of public welfare, they may appoint an agent who under the title of director of public welfare may assist them in their duties. In towns of less than 3,000 population the school physician may be designated as director.

Guardians. Two or more relatives or friends of a mentally ill person, the selectmen of the town where the person resides, or the state Department of Mental Health may file an application in the probate court to have a guardian appointed. Those who file a petition for a guardian also may petition for removal of a guardian. In towns where selectmen act as a board of public welfare, they may petition to have a guardian appointed for a spendthrift. On petition of the selectmen, board of public welfare, state Department of Mental Health or other person in interest, a probate court may appoint a temporary guardian of a minor, mentally ill person or spendthrift.

Old age assistance regulations. Rules and regulations of the state Department of Public Welfare relating to old age assistance are subject to the approval of the advisory board in the department after hearing. The selectmen and town boards of public welfare are to be given at least 15 days notice of a hearing on such approval.

ZONING

Zoning by-laws. Towns are authorized to adopt zoning by-laws by a zoning enabling act passed in 1954.

Zoning exceptions. The selectmen or a board of appeals, as the town by-laws may provide, have the right to grant special permits for zoning exceptions after a public hearing.

Changes in zoning. A by-law establishing the boundaries of zones and districts cannot be adopted until after the planning board, or the selectmen, if there is no planning board, has held a public hearing and made a report to the town meeting or unless 20 days elapse without such a report from the planning board. At the original adoption of a zoning ordinance the hearing may be held and the report submitted by a zoning board appointed by the selectmen for that purpose.

Establishment of board of appeals. Selectmen shall appoint members of a board of appeals within three months after adoption of a zoning by-law. The board is to consist of at least three members appointed for overlapping terms.

Pending appointment of the board, the selectmen shall act as such. Members may be removed for cause by the appointing authority after a hearing.

Outstanding permits. A building permit issued before the hearing on a zoning change held by the planning board, zoning board or selectmen, or prior to the issuance of a warrant for the town meeting at which such a change is considered, is not affected by the change if construction work is started within six months and proceeds to completion.

Withholding of building permit. The selectmen of a town not having a building inspector are required to withhold a building permit for the construction or alteration of a building which is in violation of the zoning by-laws. A town with zoning by-laws but with no building regulations may require that a building permit be obtained from the selectmen.

Reconsideration of amendment. If a proposed amendment to a zoning by-law receives unfavorable action at a town meeting in a town accepting a section of the zoning enabling act, it cannot again be considered for a period of two years unless its adoption is recommended by the planning board or by the selectmen in towns not having a planning board.

Reconsideration of exception. In towns accepting another section of the zoning enabling act, an appeal for variance from or application for a special exception to the zoning by-laws which have received unfavorable action cannot again be considered for a period of two years except with the consent of all members of the planning board or all of the selectmen in towns not having a planning board.

Powers And Duties Of Selectmen Relative To Public Utilities

GENERAL

Common carriers. The selectmen, as the licensing authority in a town, may adopt rules and regulations governing the operation of passenger carriers operating between fixed points which are subject to a local license. The company operating the vehicles, any railroad company operating in the town, or 20 residents of the town may petition the state Department of Public Utilities for the amendment or repeal of any such rule or regulation. The state department after a notice and hearing may amend or repeal such regulations or substitute others, and thereafter may amend or repeal such rules on its own initiative or after notice and hearing on a petition as above described. The Supreme Judicial Court and the Superior Court have jurisdiction in equity to restrain any violation of the chapter of state laws relating to common carriers of passengers by motor vehicles, on petition of the selectmen, the state Department of Public Utilities or any ten citizens affected.

ELECTRIC COMPANIES

Electric lines. Requirements for the construction of electric lines by an electric company—including the granting and transfer of locations, consent to joint locations, erection and use of wires, poles and equipment—and action by the selectmen on these matters are the same as for telephone and telegraph companies. These are discussed under the heading "Telephone Companies," since they appear in the laws under that heading.

Lines through other towns. A company, whose application for the location of an electric line extending through other towns is not granted by the selectmen within three months, may apply to the state Department of Public Utilities. The state department may grant the petition after a hearing, of which notice is given to the selectmen and to owners of real estate along the proposed location. The hearing, if requested by the selectmen, is to be held in the town where the location is sought. This provision does not apply to telephone and telegraph lines.

Regulation of electric companies. The selectmen may regulate and control all acts of an electric corporation which in any way affect the health, safety, convenience or property of the inhabitants.

Prerogative of electric company. In a town where electricity is manufactured and sold, no other party is to erect or use wires for heat or power, except those of street railway companies, without the consent of the selectmen after a notice and public hearing. Any person aggrieved by a decision of the selectmen may appeal to the state Department of Public

Utilities within 30 days, and the state department is to make a final decision after a hearing.

Complaint as to price. The state Department of Public Utilities may order a change in the price of electricity following a hearing held upon written complaint of the selectmen or 20 customers.

Rights for transmission line. An electric transmission line cannot be placed on land taken by eminent domain until the electric company has acquired from the selectmen all the necessary rights in highways, public places, parks and reservations in the towns through which the line will pass.

Conditions for bulk sales. In approving the use of wires by electric companies for furnishing electricity in bulk, the selectmen may impose such other terms as the public interest requires. The state Department of Public Utilities on an appeal may amend or add to the terms as fixed by the selectmen.

Enforcement by court. The Supreme Judicial Court and the Superior Court have jurisdiction in equity on an application of selectmen to compel the observance and restrain the violation of laws relating to electric companies.

ELECTRIC RAILROADS

Approval of location. If the state Department of Public Utilities grants a certificate for the construction of an electric railroad, the directors of the company may apply within 60 days to the selectmen of each town concerned to fix the route. The selectmen give 14 days notice of a hearing and the town clerk gives seven days notice by mail to the owners of real estate along the route. If the route is approved by the selectmen, with the agreement of the company directors and approval of the state Department of Public Utilities, the selectmen are to issue a certificate.

Disagreement on location. If the selectmen and directors agree on a route different from the first one agreed upon, or if they fail to agree within 90 days on a route which meets the approval of the state Department of Public Utilities, either the selectmen or the directors may apply to the state department within 100 days after filing of the application. After notice to the selectmen and directors, and a public hearing, the department may fix the route. Thereafter no change may be made by the directors without the approval of the state department after a hearing of which notice is given to the selectmen.

Consent to location in highway. The state Department of Public Utilities is not to locate the route of an electric railroad longitudinally in a town highway without the consent of the selectmen.

Location in highway. If the selectmen agree that an electric railroad be constructed in part on a highway or other public place they may grant the location and prescribe how the tracks shall be laid and the kind of wires, poles, rails and other appliances which shall be used. They also may impose incidental terms, conditions and obligations with approval of the state Department of Public Utilities.

Electric power lines. Requirements for the construction and location of electric power lines by an electric railroad are the same as those for telephone and telegraph companies.

Transportation of baggage. An electric railroad may act as a common carrier of baggage, express and freight to the extent approved by the selectmen on petition of the company or an interested party and after notice and hearing, subject to such regulations as may be made by the selectmen with approval of the state Department of Public Utilities.

GAS COMPANIES

Regulation of gas companies. The selectmen may regulate and control all acts of a gas company which affect health, safety, convenience or property.

Application for gas main. A gas company planning to lay a main through one or more cities and towns, whose petition for location has not been granted by the selectmen after three months, may apply to the state Department of Public Utilities. The state department is to hold a public hearing after notice to the selectmen and the abutting owners on the proposed route, and it may grant the location if it is in the public interest. If requested by the selectmen, the hearing is to be held in the town concerned.

Prerogative of gas company. In a town having a gas company in operation, no other party is to dig up a highway for the laying of gas pipes without the consent of the selectmen after a hearing.

Complaint as to price or service. On written complaint of the selectmen or of 20 customers as to the price, quality or pressure of gas sold or delivered; or the manner in which it is being stored, transported or distributed, the state Department of Public Utilities may order, after a hearing, a change in price or improvement in quality or make such orders as it may deem necessary.

RAILROADS

Approval of location. The directors of a railroad corporation which is planning to construct a railroad are required to submit a report and map to the selectmen of every town concerned. The selectmen are required to hold a hearing after two weeks notice. If the selectmen agree to the route they are to issue a certificate. If they fail to agree, the state Department of Public Utilities is to fix the route after a hearing of which the selectmen are notified.

Consent to location in highway. The route may include spurs and branches but no connecting tracks are to be laid longitudinally in a highway without the consent of the selectmen. The selectmen may impose such conditions as may be agreed upon by the directors of the railroad.

Establishment of through routes. The state Department of Public Utilities may order two or more railroad companies to establish through routes and joint rates and fares. If the selectmen act adversely upon a petition for the location of tracks necessary for a through route or if they fail to act within 60 days, any interested party may file a petition with the state Department of Public Utilities. The department may grant the location after a hearing with 14 days notice to the selectmen and others affected.

Complaint as to service. Upon written complaint by the selectmen or 20 voters concerning the service of a railroad, railway or other passenger carrier, the state Department of Public Utilities is to examine the condition and operation of the carrier.

Railroad crossing signs. The selectmen may request a railroad to erect and maintain warning signs at railroad crossings and may apply to the state Department of Public Utilities if the railroad fails to act.

Railroad stations. A railroad may relocate passenger stations and freight depots with the written approval of the selectmen and the state Department of Public Utilities.

Eminent domain by railroad. A railroad corporation seeking to take land by eminent domain is to file a description with the state Department of Public Utilities and to submit a certified copy of the proposed location with the selectmen of every town concerned. Selectmen are to hold a hearing after two weeks notice. If the selectmen and railroad directors agree, the selectmen fix the location, issue a certificate and report their action to the state department.

Disagreement on location. If the selectmen and the railroad corporation fail to agree within 60 days after submission of the location to the selectmen, the railroad directors may petition the state Department of Public Utilities within another 60 days to fix the location. The state department is to notify the selectmen of a hearing and fix the location within 90 days.

Change of direction. A railroad corporation is not to locate a railroad outside of the limits of the route fixed by agreement with the selectmen without their written consent. If they do not consent within 60 days, the railroad may petition the state Department of Public Utilities for a change of direction.

Location near State House. A steam railroad is not to be located within three miles of the State House without the written consent of the state Department of Public Utilities and the selectmen of any town where a location is sought.

STREET RAILWAYS

Approval of location. Upon the petition of a street railway company for an original location of tracks, the selectmen are to hold a hearing after 14 days notice and further notice to members of the legislature representing the town. The selectmen may grant the location or any part of it and may decide where the tracks shall be laid and the kind of rails, poles, wires and other appliances which shall be used. They also may impose other terms, conditions and obligations incidental to the objects of a street railway company.

Amendment of location. The state Department of Public Utilities must approve the location after a hearing. If it requires an alteration, the state department shall notify the selectmen who may amend the location. If the alteration involves a change in route, notice is to be given and a hearing held in the same manner as for an original application.

Alteration of location. Upon petition of a street railway or any interested party, selectmen may alter the location of tracks after a hearing. The alteration is to be made at such time and at the expense of such parties as the selectmen may determine. This also requires approval of the state Department of Public Utilities after a hearing. If the department requires an amendment, it is to notify the selectmen. They may amend the alteration. But if it involves a change of route, a hearing is to be held as for the original application. The street railway is to file its acceptance with the selectmen.

Location on private land. A street railway, after approval by the selectmen, may petition the state Department of Public Utilities for authority to construct part of its railway on private land off the highways, and the petition may be granted after a notice and hearing.

Taking of private land. A street railway may apply to the selectmen for approval of the taking by eminent domain of private land for construction of a railway. This also requires a certificate from the state Department of Public Utilities after a notice and hearing. A street railway taking private land by eminent domain is subject to numerous provisions of the laws which are cited in the statute concerned with the subject.

Extension of tracks. Upon petition of a street railway or of 50 voters, selectmen may grant a location for extension of tracks after a notice and hearing. This also requires approval of the state Department of Public Utilities after a notice and hearing by the department. If the department requires an alteration in the location it is to notify the selectmen. They then may amend the application for extension. If the alteration involves a change in route, a hearing must be held as required for an original application. The street railway is to file its acceptance of the location with the selectmen.

Temporary tracks. The several boards, departments, and commissioners authorized by law to grant locations to street railway companies may grant petitions without a hearing for the temporary location of tracks in order to avoid interruptions of service, and they may place a time limit on their use. If a bridge is to be repaired, selectmen may grant a petition for a temporary location of tracks and are to file a certificate with the town clerk that it is in the public interest. The company must file an acceptance of the location with the selectmen.

Discontinuance of tracks. If a street railway company voluntarily discontinues the use of tracks for a period of six months, the selectmen may order their removal. The company is under no obligation to pay any part of the expense of resurfacing. If a company discontinues the use of tracks without excuse and refuses a request of the selectmen to operate, the selectmen, if they are so authorized by vote of the town, may petition the Supreme Judicial Court to compel the use of the tracks.

Temporary discontinuance. The selectmen may order a street railway to discontinue temporarily the use of any track if the public safety or convenience so requires.

Revocation of location. After one year following the date of opening of a street railway, the selectmen may revoke the location for good and sufficient reasons stated in the order. Unless the company consents to the action within 30 days, the order is not valid until approved by the state Department of Public Utilities after a hearing. If the order is approved, the selectmen may direct the removal of the railway. The company is under no obligation to pay for any part of the resurfacing of streets.

Opening of highways. A street railway company may open any highway or bridge in order to make repairs to the railway. Selectmen are to issue the necessary permits in towns where permits are required.

Electric power lines. Requirements for the construction and location of electric power lines by a street railway are the same as for telephone and telegraph companies.

Transportation of baggage. A street railway may be a common carrier of baggage, express and freight, subject to rules and regulations prescribed by the selectmen. If the selectmen fail to act in 30 days on a petition for approval, the company may apply to the state Department of Public Utilities. The state department may make a final decision within 30 days after a hearing.

Transportation of road materials. A street railway company, with the consent of the selectmen, may transport snow, ice, stones, gravel or street sweepings over its tracks; as well as any materials for constructing, grading or improving a street. The company may make contracts with a town for the transportation of such materials.

Regulation by selectmen. The selectmen may establish regulations as to the manner, extent and use of tracks, rate of speed, and the number and use of cars. Such regulations are subject to approval, revision or alteration by the state Department of Public Utilities. Selectmen are to send a copy of the rules and regulations to the company and the state Department of Public Utilities before the first day of September of each year. The department may amend the regulations on petition of the company after a hearing.

Snow removal. Selectmen are to establish regulations for the clearance of snow from street railway tracks and its removal from the highway.

Warning signals. Selectmen may establish regulations requiring a motorman or conductor to give notice or warning of the approach of street cars. Such regulations are subject to approval by the state Department of Public Utilities.

Change in rates. The state Department of Public Utilities is to give notice to selectmen upon the filing of a petition by a street railway for a change in rates.

Enforcement by courts. The Supreme Judicial Court and Superior Court have jurisdiction in equity on a petition of selectmen or street railway to compel the observance and restrain the violation of laws relating to street railways. The courts may review, annul or amend rulings of any state department or commission.

TELEPHONE COMPANIES

Telephone and telegraph. The provisions of law which are concerned with telephone companies apply also to telegraph companies.

Erection of wires. Requirements relating to the construction of lines, including the granting and transfer of locations, consent to joint locations, erection and use of wires, poles and equipment, and action by the selectmen on these matters apply alike to telephone and telegraph companies, electric companies, electric railroads and street railways.

Application for line. A telephone or telegraph company is to petition the selectmen in writing for permission to construct a line on, under or across a highway. After a public hearing, with seven days notice by the selectmen or town clerk to owners of real property along the proposed route, the selectmen may grant a location. They also may specify where poles, piers or abutments are to be placed and the number and height of wires and cables. After erection of the line, the selectmen may permit an increase in the number or height of wires and alteration of the poles, piers or abutments.

Joint locations. On petition of two or more companies, the selectmen may grant joint or identical locations for the construction of new lines after a hearing of which seven days notice is given by the selectmen or town clerk.

Transfer of locations. On petition of two or more companies having locations in the town, the selectmen may transfer any location from one company to another without a hearing. They also may authorize a company to attach its wires and fixtures to the equipment of another company, or may grant them joint or identical locations to be used in common.

Joint use of equipment. Selectmen may authorize the attachment of the wires and fixtures of a street railway or electric company to the poles and equipment of another company, and they may grant joint or identical locations to be used in common by such companies and another owner. This is not to extend a location already granted to a street railway or electric railway company.

Certification of action. In cases where a notice and hearing are required, the town clerk, chairman of the selectmen or a majority of the selectmen are to certify in the books of the town clerk that the order was adopted after notice and hearing.

Use of highways. Selectmen may permit telephone, telegraph and television lines to be laid under a highway. They may establish reasonable regulations for the erection of all such lines or for electric lines other than for street railways by every person having authority to install them, including all lines owned by the town. The selectmen are required to give written notice to any person using a line in violation of regulations. The Supreme Judicial Court or Superior Court may enjoin their construction or order their alteration or removal.

Lines to other towns. Any town regulations which are imposed in a grant of location for an electric line extending to another city or town are required to have the approval of the state Department of Public Utilities.

Private lines. Selectmen may authorize citizens to establish and maintain poles, wires, and other telephone and telegraph apparatus in accordance with law. They may authorize a person to erect private telephone and telegraph lines and private lines for the transmission of electricity for heat, light or power on such terms and conditions as they may prescribe. Upon the construction of any such line, the poles and structures on the highways are to become the property of the town and are under the control of the selectmen. Selectmen may require their alteration or order their removal after a notice and hearing.

Town wires. A town may attach wires for its own use to private poles and structures and may permit other persons, on prescribed terms and conditions, to attach wires for their own use to private poles or poles erected by the town.

Equipment in private ways. On petition of a company, the selectmen may grant a location in a private way which has been accepted as a public highway for the use of equipment which previously had been located there.

Complaint as to service. Upon a written complaint relative to the service or charges for service of a telephone or telegraph company by the selectmen or 20 customers, the state Department of Public Utilities is to hold a public hearing.

Underground lines. An officer or board authorized to grant locations for underground conduits under a special law or agreement is to hold a public hearing before giving permission for the placing or removal of such lines. Owners of real estate along the location may appeal within 30 days to the state Department of Public Utilities. The department is to give a final decision after a hearing.

Cutting of wires. When company wires must be cut in order to move a building or for other good reason, and after proper petition by the party concerned the company neglects or refuses to do so, the selectmen in a town having no inspector of wires shall cause the wires to be cut, disconnected or removed. The town may collect from the company its expenses in doing so.

WATER COMPANIES

Prerogative of water company. In a town where a water company exists, no other person or company is to dig in highways for the laying of water pipes without the consent of the selectmen after a notice and hearing. Any person aggrieved by such a decision of the selectmen may appeal to the state Department of Public Utilities within 30 days, and the department may render a decision after a hearing.

Water for fire protection. A town in which an aqueduct is located may install conductors in the pipes for the purpose of drawing free water in the event of fire. If the selectmen consider it necessary, they may direct the engineers of the fire department to request that fittings for hydrants be installed by the company. If the company neglects to comply within two weeks, the engineers of the fire department may make such connections at the expense of the town.

Water meter testing. Persons using water supplied by a meter are entitled to have the meter examined and tested. If water is supplied by a water company, the test is to be made by a competent person designated by the selectmen.

Reference To General Laws Concerning Selectmen

References are to the General Laws of Massachusetts, as amended. The first number refers to the chapter and the second number to the section.

A

Accountant
    Appointment of accountant 41-55
    Assistant accountant 41-49A
    Notice of expended appropriations 41-58
    Report to selectmen 41-58
    Vacancy 41-40
Accounts
    Inspection by selectmen 41-52, 5-164-56
    Report of state audit 44-39
    Request for state audit 44-35
    Request for state investigation 44-46A
Advertising of town 40-6A
Agent of public welfare board 41-32, 32A
Airports
    Airport commission 90-51E
    Approaches, acquisition 90-40G, 40I
    Approaches, regulations 90-40A, 40B, 40C, 40I
    Establishment by town 90-51D
    Joint airports, establishment 90-51N
Alcoholic beverages
    Appeal of applicant to state 138-67
    Licenses, consumed on premises 138-12
    Licenses, consumed off premises 138-15
    Licenses, pharmacy 138-29 to 30F
    Licenses, seasonal 138-17
    Licenses, special, beer and wine 138-14
    Licenses, taverns 138-11A
    Number of licenses 138-17
    Prohibition of sale during riot 138-68
    Referendum on tavern sales 138-11A
    Regulation of sales 138-23
    Report on licenses to state 138-10A
    Selectmen as licensing authority 138-1
    Temporary summer population 138-17
Animal inspectors, nomination 129-15
Anniversary, date of settlement 40-5 (27)
Appropriations
    Estimates of appropriations 41-59, 60
    Exceeding in emergency 44-31
    Legality 40-53
    Liabilities not to exceed 44-31
    Report on condition 41-58
    Transfers of appropriations 44-33B
    Unpaid bills 44-64
Aqueduct companies
    Digging in highways 165-20
    Furnishing water for fires 165-26

Armories
      Rental of armory to state 33-119
      Sale of armory to state 33-127
Art commission, appointment 41-38
Assessors
      Appointment or election 41-1, 21, 24, 25, 26
      Compensation for service to districts 41-108B
      Employment of counsel 41-26A
      Failure to perform duties 41-27
      Number of assessors 41-1, 24, 25, 26
      Selectmen as assessors 41-20, 21
      Temporary, by state appointment 41-27
Audit
      Annual audit 44-40
      Regional school district 71-16E
      Request for state audit 44-35
      Trust accounts 41-53
Auditor
      Abolition of office 41-55
      Assistant auditor 41-49A
      Vacancy 41-40, 49
Automobiles, second hand dealers 140-66
Awards for employee suggestions 40-5 (43)

B

Ballot clerks, appointment in certain towns 54-19
Ballots, and ballot boxes, regulations 50-7
Beach district, establishment 40-12B
Bells and whistles, regulation of use by employers 149-175
Betterments 80-1, 80A-1
Bicycles, registration 85-11A
Bills and payrolls
      Approval of selectmen 41-52
      Municipal lighting plant, approval 164-56
Bills, unpaid bills of prior years 44-64
Board of appeals, subdivision 41-81Z
Board of appeals, zoning 40A-14
Board of election commissioners 51-16A
Board of health, selectmen as board in certain towns 41-1
Board of public works
      Acceptance of 1953 statute 41-69C
      Appointment of superintendent 41-69E
      Election of board 41-69D
      Powers of board 41-69D
      Selectmen as board under 1920 statute 41-21
Board of survey, selectmen as board in certain towns 41-73
Boards, open meetings 39-23A, 23B, 23C
Boards, vacancies in boards 41-11
Bonds and notes
      Interest rate 41-22
      Issuance 44-16, 24
Bootblacks, regulation 101-19
Borrowing
      Anticipation of reimbursements 44-6A
      Anticipation of school grants 71-26D
      Before town meeting 44-5
      Bonds and notes 44-16, 24
      School deficiency 71-34
Boundary line
      Boundary markers 42-4
      Boundary with other states 42-5
      Penalty for neglect 42-6
      Perambulation of line 42-2, 3

Boxing matches, acceptance by town 147-49, 50
Bridges
    Charles River bridges, rebuilding 92-69
    Drawbridge maintenance 84-2
Budget, submission by selectmen 39-16
Building inspection, enforcement in places of assembly 143-3A
Building inspection district, appointment of building inspector 143-3
Building inspector, appointment in certain towns 145-49
Building permits
    Effect of zoning on prior permits 40A-11
    Withholding of permits 40A-12
Buildings
    Dangerous, abatement or removal 139-1, 143-5
    Destruction in case of fire 48-3
    Fireproofing requirements, exceptions 143-4
    Moving in highways, permit 85-18
    Request for state inspection 143-13
    Unsafe, committee to survey 143-8
    Use for explosives 148-13, 14
    Use for fireworks manufacture 148-12
Busses
    Regulation by selectmen 159A-12
    Selectmen as licensing authority 159A-1, 4
    Violation of regulations, petition to enjoin 159A-15

C

Cadet engineers, training by municipal light boards 164-69B, 69D
Carriages, regulation by selectmen 40-22
Caucus
    Notice of date 53-82
    Polling places 53-82
    Town nominations 53-121
    Voting lines 53-93
Cemeteries
    Appointment of commissioners 41-21, 114-27
    Approval of employees 114-27
    Control by selectmen 114-27
    Investment of funds 114-25
    Land taking 114-11
    Private cemeteries, care 114-16
Census, duty of selectmen 9-7
Chairman of selectmen
    Appointment of commission on children's health camps 111-62B
    Appointment of committee on employee suggestions 40-5 (43)
    Certifies action on location of wires 166-22
    Certifies election of clerk in certain cases 41-19A
    Duties as to beach district 40-12B
    Duties as to building inspection district 143-3
    Duties as to grade crossing changes 159-80
    Duties as to health camp board 111-62B
    Member union health camp board 111-62F
    Member veterans' services district board 115-11
    Member hospital evaluation board 111-91
    Notified of court order on pollution appeal 111-163
    Notified of hearing on public health nuisance 111-135
    Presiding election officer in certain cases 54-18
    Presiding at town meeting 39-14
    Receives regional school audit 71-16E
    Reporting of automobile accidents 90-29
    Sunday work permits 136-9
    War memorial trustee 41-105
Charitable corporations, investigation prior to incorporation 180-5

Chief of fire department
    Appointment by commissioner 41-101
    Appointment by selectmen 41-21, 48-42
    Powers in certain towns 48-42
    Service as forest warden 48-43
Chief of police department
    Appointment by commissioner 41-101
    Appointment by selectmen 41-21, 97, 97A
    Powers in certain towns 41-97, 97A
Children
    Commercial entertainments, participation 149-104, 105
    Eyeglasses, purchase for school children 40-5 (40)
    Health camp districts 111-62F
    Health camps, establishment 111-62B
Civil Defense, Acts of 1950, 639-11, 13
Collector
    Accounting by collector 60-94
    Approval of bond 41-20; 60-13
    Compensation for service to districts 41-108B
    Indemnification 41-43A
    Removal by commissioner of corporations 41-39B
    Removal by selectmen 60-96
    Special tax collector 60-14
    Vacancy 41-40
Commission of public safety 41-21
Commissioner of health, appointment 111-26B
Commissioner of public safety
    Appointment by selectmen 41-101
    Appointment of deputy as police chief 41-101
    Appointment of deputy fire chiefs 41-101
Commissioners of trust funds
    Selectmen as such in small towns 41-45A
    Vacancy 41-45
Conservation commissions 40-86
Constables
    Application and investigation 41-91B
    Appointment by selectmen 41-91A
    Approval of bond 41-92
    Motor vehicle constables 90-29
    Shellfish constables 130-98
Corporations
    Charitable, investigation 180-5
    Electric (see Electric companies)
    Electric railway (see Electric railways)
    Gas (see Gas companies)
    Railroad (see Railroads)
    Street railway (see Street railways)
    Telephone (see Telephone companies)
    Telegraph (see Telephone companies)
    Water (see Water companies)
Counsel
    Employment for assessors 41-26A
    Employment for treasurer 41-43A
County commissioners, selectmen to receive report 35-27
County finances, selectmen may request report 35-28
Custodian of landing places 88-14
Custodian of property acquired by foreclosure 60-77B
Custodian of state reports 40-48, 78-7

D

Damages
    Award of damages for corporation 79-10
    Failure to pay by corporation 79-42
    Liability for highway defects 84-15, 18, 19

Development and industrial commission 40-8A
Disaster relief, providing of necessities in distress or emergency 40-19
Districts
- Agreement for payment to towns 41-108B
- Beach district 40-12B
- Building inspection district 143-3
- Children's health camp district 111-62F
- Greenhead fly control district 252-24
- Plumbing inspection district 142-10
- Public beach district 40-12B
- Public welfare district 117-44
- Regional health district 111-27B
- Regional planning district 40B-3
- Regional school district 71-14 to 16
- Transportation area 161-143 to 146
- Veterans' services district 115-10, 11, 12
- Wire inspection district 166-32

Dog officer
- Appointment by selectmen 140-151
- Performance of duties by S.P.C.A. 140-151

Dogs
- Appraisal of damage done by dogs 140-161, 165
- Investigation of complaint 140-157
- Order to muzzle dogs 140-167, 168
- Regulation of kennels 140-137C
- Restraint of dangerous dogs 140-160

Drivers of vehicles and fire apparatus, approval by selectmen 40-5 (1)
Dumping ground, assignment by board of health 111-150A
Dutch elm disease, suppression 132-13

E

Election commissioners, appointment 51-16A
Elections
- Ballot boxes, additional 54-67A
- Ballot clerks, in certain towns 54-19
- Ballots for selectmen and other officers 41-9
- Caucus (see Caucus)
- Election commissioners 51-16A
- Election officers 54-12, 13
- Election officers, tellers 54-21
- Election officers, vacancy 54-14, 16, 16A
- Examination of records 54-111
- Hours of voting 54-64
- False election record, penalty 56-19
- Polling places, change in place 54-24
- Polling places, designation 54-24
- Polling places, display of flag 54-25A
- Powers of selectmen 54-18
- Record of election, certification 54-111
- Registrars of voters 51-15, 16, 16A
- Regulation of ballots and ballot boxes 50-7
- Selectmen as registrars in small towns 51-16
- Special, for certain county officers 54-143
- Special, for county commissioners 54-144
- Special, for referendum on tavern liquor sales 138-11A
- Special, for representative in Congress 54-140
- Special, for state representative 54-141
- Tellers, appointment 54-21
- Voting machines 54-34
- Voting precincts, division 54-7A
- Voting precincts, establishment 54-6
- Voting precincts, map 54-8

Voting precincts, for representative town meeting 43A-3
Voting precincts, revision 54-7
Warrant for election 39-10; 54-63, 64
Electric companies
    Complaint as to price 164-93
    Construction of lines 164-71; 166-21, 22
    Electric power lines (see Electric lines)
    Erection or use of wires other than by company 164-87, 88
    Lines through other towns 166-27, 28
    Regulation 164-75, 90
    Transmission line, rights in highways 164-72
    Violation of laws, application to courts 164-91
Electric lines
    Action by selectmen, certification 166-22
    Construction 166-21, 22
    Joint or identical locations 166-22
    Location of lines 166-22
    Private lines, regulation 164-24
    Regulation 166-25
    Removal of unused poles and wires 86-7
    Transfer of locations 166-22
    Use of highways 166-22 to 26
Electric railroads
    Carrying of baggage and freight 162-14
    Construction 162-8
    Electric power lines (see Electric lines)
    Route, application 162-8
    Route, determination 162-9
    Regulation 162-10
    Use of highways 162-10
Electricity
    Manufacture by street railway 161-45
    Purchase by town from street railway 161-52, 54
Emergency expenditures 40-6, 53; 44-31
Eminent domain
    Award of damages 79-7, 10
    Conservation and recreation 132A-3A
    Judicial proceedings 80A-1
    Land taking for airports 90-40G, 40I, 51G
    Land taking for ditches and drains 83-4
    Land taking for highways 82-22, 24; 84-10
    Land taking for low land areas 252-15, 18
    Land taking for parking lots 40-22B
    Land taking for sewage disposal 83-6
    Land taking for sewers 83-1
    Manner of land taking 79-1; 80A-1
    Railroad corporation 160-80
    Selectmen, powers 40-14; 79-2
    Street railway company 161-58, 59, 129
    Water supply 40-39B
Estimates
    Appropriations 41-59, 60
    Municipal lighting plant 164-57
Executive secretary to selectmen 41-23A
Eyeglasses, for school children 40-5 (40)

F

Fees, report of town officers 40-21 (13)
Fence viewers, appointment 49-1
Field drivers, appointment 49-22
Finance committee 39-16
Finance laws, report of violations 44-62

Firearms, sale or rental 140-22
Fire chief (see Chief of fire department)
Fire department
 Assistance to other towns 48-59A
 Engineers 48-45, 46
 Establishment 48-42
 Under civil service 48-44
Fire district, establishment 48-62
Fire engines
 Enginemen 48-29, 30
 Enginemen for private engines 48, 32, 33
 Hosemen 48-35
Firemen, indemnification of retired firemen 41-100B
Firemen, permission for association or club 48-84
Firewards, appointment 48-1
Fireworks
 Bond for storage 148-40
 Permit for manufacture 148-12
Fish and game
 Acquisition of properties, approval 131-25
 Occupation of ponds, approval 131-14
Fish traps, authorization 130-29
Fish weighers, appointment 41-88, 89
Forest
 Acquisition of forest land 45-20
 Control by town forest commission 45-21
 Forest commission, appointment 45-21
Forest fires
 Payment for forest fires 48-12
 Supervision of expenditures 48-24
Forest wardens
 Appointment by selectmen 48-8
 Fire chief as forest warden 48-43
Furnaces, iron and glass making, regulation 140-115, 116, 119

G

Garbage disposal (see also Incinerator)
 Contracts 40-4
 Dumping grounds, approval 111-150A
 Incinerator, approval of site 111-150A
Gas companies
 Application to lay main 164-70A
 Complaint as to price or quality 164-93
 Complaint as to storage or distribution 164-105A
 Digging in highways 164-70
 Laying of pipes other than by company 164-86
 Regulation 164-75
Gasoline, regulation of storage and use 148-9, 13
Grade crossings
 Abolition, agreement 159-80
 Abolition, petition 159-65
 Abolition, by street railways 161-129
 Alteration, agreement 159-80
 Alteration, application 159-59
 Alteration, procedure 159-61 to 64
 Alteration of highway by railroad 160-100
 Authorization of crossing 160-102
 Warning signs, request by selectmen 160-141
Guardian, petition for appointment 201-6, 8, 13A, 14
Gymnasium, control by selectmen 40-5 (25)

H

Harbor master
    Appointment 102-19
    Assistant harbor master 102-19
Health
    Advisory council 111-26C
    Dangerous disease, protection 111-104
    Selectmen as board of health 41-21, 102
Health camps
    Children's health camps, establishment 111-62B
    Union health camp districts 111-62F
Health commissioner, appointment 111-26B
Health department, advisory council 111-26C
Health district, regional, methods of creating 111-27B
Health inspector, appointment 41-102, 102A
Health nuisances
    Notice of hearing on petition 111-135
    Petition for abatement 111-134
Highway safety activities 40-7A
Highway surveyor
    Limits of districts 41-62
    Powers 41-62
    Temporary surveyor 41-40
Highways
    Acceptance by town meeting 82-23, 27
    Alteration by railroad at crossing 160-100
    Alteration of water courses 84-9
    Alteration for water supply 40-39C
    Boundaries and measurements 82-23, 32
    Boundary markers 86-1
    Coasting on designated highways 85-10A
    Closing during construction 84-15, 24
    Contract with state 81-15, 28
    Contribution to cost of state highway 81-10
    County commissioners, powers 82-1, 2, 26, 27; 160-104
    Damages resulting from defects 84-15, 18, 19
    Digging by gas companies 164-70
    Digging for pipes by aqueduct companies 165-20
    Digging for pipes by certain corporations 158-12, 14
    Digging for water pipes, other than by water company 165-8, 9
    Eminent domain 82-22, 24; 84-10
    Effect of official map on construction 41-81G
    Federal aid state-local highways 81-29A
    Gravel pits, acquisition for road materials 82-38
    Land taking 82-22, 24; 84-10
    Laying out by county 82-1, 2
    Laying out by town 82-17, 21, 22
    Layout across railroad 160-104
    Layout of railroad across highway 160-102
    Liability for injury or damages 84-15, 18, 19, 24
    Naming of streets 85-3A, 3B
    Neglect of selectmen to build 82-26
    Neglect of town to accept 82-27
    Obstruction by railroad at crossing 160-106
    Petition for state funds 81-27
    Petition for state highway 81-4
    Pipes, laying of pipes in highway 82-25
    Railroad tracks in highway, approval 160-22
    Regulation of coasting 85-10A
    Removal of unused poles and wires 86-7
    Repairs by railroad at crossing 160-106
    Repairs by street railway 161-89
    Selectmen, jurisdiction 82-17, 21, 22
    Snow removal, additional liabilities 44-13

Snow removal, agreements 84-5A
State funds for local highways 81-26; 90-34 (2) (a)
State trails or paths, town contribution 132-39
State work on local highways 81-24, 25, 26
Temporary repairs on private ways 40-6G
Tree planting and removal 87-2, 4, 5
Use by electric companies 164-72
Use for electric wires 166-22 to 26
Use by electric railroads 162-10
Use by private railroads 160-245
Use for private wires 166-23, 24
Use by railroads 160-22
Use by street railways 161-7, 45
Water course, relocation of 84-9
Water supply work, direction of selectmen 40-39C

Hospitals
County hospital, town share of cost 111-91
Free bed, certification 111-74
Location in town 111-75

Housing authority
Open meetings 39-23A, 23B, 23C
Organization 121-26K
Removal of members 121-26M
Temporary members 121-26K

I

Improvement associations, care of public grounds 45-12
Incinerator 40-5 (19A); 92-9A
Approval of site 111-150A
Authority of town 40-5 (19A)
Contract by town 40-4
Metropolitan district 92-9A
Indemnification of collector 41-43A
Indemnification of employees 41-100A
Indemnification of retired policemen and firemen 41-100B
Indemnification of treasurer 41-43A
Insect pest control
Financial liability 132-11, 14, 17
Local superintendent 132-13, 25
State assistance 132-16
Trees on private land 132-26F, 26G
Inspector of animals 129-15
Inspector of buildings 145-49; 143-6; 145-49
Inspector of health 41-102, 102A
Inspector of lime 94-262
Inspector of milk 94-33
Inspector of unsafe buildings 143-8
Inspector of wires 166-32
Insurance
Group insurance for employees 32B-1, 2, 3
Group insurance in small towns 32B-11
Liability, for drivers of vehicles 40-5 (1)
Interest rate on bonds and notes 44-22
Investigation of town departments by selectmen 41-23B

J

Jurors
Drawing by selectmen 234-19
Drawing at town meeting 234-22
List of persons qualified 234-4
Printing of jury list 234-5
Selection of jurors 234-7

L

Labor disputes
    Arbitration, approval of fees 150-9
    Strike or lockout, notice to state 150-9
Land conveyance 40-15
Land, restrictions on use for inflammables 148-13, 14
Land taking, by eminent domain 40-14
Land transfer 40-15A
Landing places or wharves
    Appointment of custodian 88-14
    Establishment and regulation 88-14
Legislative acts, petition for revocation of acceptance 4-4A
Liabilities
    Additional, for snow removal 44-13
    Appropriations not to be exceeded 44-31
    Incurring prior to appropriations 44-13
Library treasurer, approval of bond 78-10
Licenses
    Alcoholic beverages 138-12, 15
    Amateur sports (Sunday) 136-27
    Amusement park activities (Sunday) 136-4A
    Amusements, public 140-181
    Auctioneers 100-2
    Auctioneers, for bankrupt or insolvent goods 100-18
    Automobiles, second hand sales 140-159
    Basketball games (Sunday) 136-21
    Bathing suits, rental 140-194, 195
    Beach resort activities (Sunday) 136-4A
    Beverages, non-intoxicating 140-21A
    Billiard tables 140-177
    Boats, power 140-189
    Boats, rental 140-194, 195
    Bootblacks 101-19
    Bowling alleys 140-177
    Bowling alleys (Sunday) 136-4B
    Buildings, fireproofing exceptions 143-4
    Busses, other than interstate 159A-1
    Cabins, overnight 140-32A to 32E
    Carousels 140-186
    Charitable organizations, temporary sales 101-33
    Clubs, for food and beverages 140-21E
    Coffee houses 140-47
    Concerts, in restaurants 140-183A
    Dances, in restaurants 140-183A
    Dancing schools 140-185H
    Employment offices 140-42
    Entertainments (Sunday) 136-4
    Exhibitions 140-181
    Exhibitions, in restaurants 140-183A
    Explosives, manufacture or storage 148-13
    Ferris wheels 140-186
    Fire fighting exhibitions 140-186
    Firearms, sale or rental 140-122
    Fireworks, manufacture 148-12
    Frozen desserts, confectionery, soda and fruit (Sunday) 136-7
    Furnaces, iron and glass making 140-115
    Games and sports, outdoor (Sunday) 136-21
    Inclined railway 140-186
    Innholder 140-2, 9
    Intelligence offices 140-42
    Junk dealers 140-54, 55, 56
    Lodging houses, five or more persons 140-23, 30
    Lunch carts 140-49
    Milk 94-52, 53

    Parking lots 148-56
    Passenger carriers, motor vehicles 159A-1
    Pawnbrokers 140-70
    Peddlers of certain commodities 101-17
    Petroleum products, storage and use 148-13
    Picnic groves 140-188
    Pinball machines 140-177A
    Pistols, carrying 140-131
    Pistols, purchasing or renting 140-131A
    Pistols, sale or rental 140-122
    Pool tables 140-177
    Roller skating rinks 140-186
    Sales by minors 101-19
    Second hand articles 140-54, 55
    Second hand motor vehicles   4A-140-159
    Shellfish 130-52, 55, 57
    Shooting galleries 140-56A
    Shows, public 140-181
    Shows, public shows in restaurants 140-183A
    Sippio tables 140-177
    Smoke, emission 140-132, 133
    Stables 111-158
    Steam engines for saw mills 140-115
    Steamboats 140-191
    Sunday entertainments 136-4 et seq.
    Sunday work or labor 136-9
    Taverns, sale of beverages 138-11A
    Tea houses 140-47
    Theatrical exhibitions 140-181
    Trailer camps 140-32A to 32E
    Transient vendors 101-5
    Used car sales 140-159
    Vehicles 40-22
    Veterans posts, temporary sales 101-33
    Victuallers 140-2, 9
Licensing authority
    Alcoholic liquors 138-1
    Fire prevention 148-1
    Local licenses 140-1
    Passenger carriers 159A-4
Lighting (see Municipal light board)
Loans, on collateral security, inspection of records 140-87
Lockup, appointment of keeper 40-35, 36
Lodging houses
    Definition, for five or more persons 140-23
    Inspection of houses 140-25
    Inspection of register 140-28
    Order to keep register 140-27, 28
Low lands and swamps
    Drainage and improvement 252-1, 4A
    Petition of land owner for access 252-21, 22, 23

M

Manager of municipal lighting 164-56
Map, hearing on change in official map 41-81F
Market, petition for public market place 40-10
Measurers of leather, appointment 95-1
Measurers of lumber 96-7, 8
Measurers of wood and bark 94-296, 297, 300
Militia
    Call in case of catastrophe 33-42
    Call in case of riot 33-41

Expense of town 33-49
Rental of armory and facilities to state 33-119
Sale of armory and facilities to state 33-127
Unorganized militia 33-55
Milk
    Collectors of milk samples 94-33, 34
    Frozen desserts, license from board of health 94-65H, 65I
    Inspector of milk, appointment 94-33
    Milk dealers, permit from board of health 94-43
    Milk license, issued by inspector of milk 94-52, 53
Minors, regulation of sales by minors 101-19
Moderator, absence at town meeting 39-14
Motor vehicles
    Junk license 140-58
    Law enforcement 90-29
    Off-street parking 40-22B
    Parking lots 148-56
    Parking meters 40-22A
    Speed regulations 90-18
    Use of certain highways 90-18
    Used car sales, licensing 140-57 to 66
Municipal light board
    Election by town 164-55
    Selectmen as municipal light board 41-21
    Training and employment of cadet engineers 164-69B, 69D
Municipal lighting
    Bills and payrolls, approval 164-56
    Books and accounts, submitted to state 164-63
    Estimates of income and expenses 164-57
    Exemption from established standard for gas 164-107
    Manager of municipal lighting 164-56
    Municipal lighting plant, management 164-56
    Report to state department 164-63

N

Nominations by town caucus 53-121
Nuisances
    Abatement 139-3
    Dangerous buildings 139-1; 143-5
    Near public gatherings 139-18
    Public health nuisances 111-134 to 136
    Smoke nuisances 140-132, 135

O

Open meetings 39-23A, 23B, 23C

P

Park commissioners, selectmen as commissioners 41-21; 45-2
Parking lots, licensing 148-56
Parking meters, installation 40-22A
Parking, off-street parking lots 40-22B
Passenger carriers
    Complaint as to service 159-24
    Petition to restrain violation 159A-15
    Regulation 159A-1, 12
Pawnbrokers, inspection of premises 140-73
Petroleum products
    Laying of pipes 40-43A
    Regulation of manufacture and storage 148-9, 13

Planning
    Conservation commissions 40-8C
    Planning board 41-81A
    Planning law 41-70 to 81J
    Regional planning law 40B-1 to 7
    Report and recommendations 41-81C
    Selectmen as planning board 41-81A, 81B
Playgrounds
    Establishment 45-14, 16
    Management 45-14
    Referendum on providing 45-16
    Temporary, lease in certain towns 45-17
    Use of property for other town purposes 45-14
Plumbing inspector, approval of compensation 142-9
Police department
    Establishment 41-97, 97A
    Rules and regulations 41-97, 97A
    Weapons, authorized 41-98
Police officers
    Appointment 41-96, 97, 97A
    Hours of duty 147-16
    Indemnification of retired officers 41-100B
    Reserve force 147-13A, 13C
    Service in another town 41-99
    Service on federal reservations 147-1A
Political committees
    Nomination of election officers 54-12
    Notice of caucus date 53-82
Polling places (see Elections)
Pollution
    Appeal from order of state department 111-163
    Application to enjoin violation 111-169
    Permits authorized by state department 111-160
    Petition to state department 111-162
    Shellfish purification plant 130-76 to 79
Pound keeper, appointment 49-22
Private ways, snow removal 40-6C
Process, service in action against town 223-37
Property
    Conveyance of land 40-15
    Control by selectmen 40-3
    Lease by selectmen 40-3
    Power to hold, lease and sell 40-3
    Taking by eminent domain 40-14; 79-2
Public domain, acquisition 45-20
Public market, petition 40-10
Public safety commissioner, appointment 41-101
Public utility employees, selectmen not to ask appointment 271-40
Public welfare
    Old age assistance regulations, notice of hearing 118A-10
    Public welfare agent 41-32, 32A
    Public welfare district 117-44
    Selectmen as board of public welfare 41-20, 21, 31
Public works board (see Board of public works)
Purchasing agent, appointment 41-103
Purchasing department establishment 41-103

R

Railroad crossings (see Grade crossings)
Railroads
    Alteration of highways at crossing 160-100
    Bridge maintenance and repair, application 159-84
    Bridge repair at crossing of highway 160-106

Complaint as to service 159-24
Construction, agreement on route 160-20, 21, 80
Construction, change in route 160-86
Construction, eminent domain 160-80
Construction, hearing 160-19
Electric (see Electric railroads)
Layout across highway 160-102
Location within three miles of state house 160-77
Private railroads, use of highways 160-245
Station relocation 160-129
Street railways (see Street railways)
Through routes, approval 159-21
Tracks in highway, approval 160-22
Use of highways 160-22
Warning signs at crossings 160-141
Reclamation district, petition for organization 252-4A, 5
Recognizance, authorization 40-45
Records, control of state books and records 40-48
Recreation center, establishment 45-14
Redevelopment authority
    Acquisition of housing project 121-26QQ
    Organization of authority 121-26QQ
    Temporary members 121-26QQ
Redevelopment project, application for approval 121-26KK
Regional health district 111-27B
Regional planning law 40B-1 to 7
Regional school district
    Agreement 71-14B
    Audit 71-16E
    Authorization of debt 71-16
    Establishment 71-15
    Operating funds 71-16B
    Recommendation for district 71-14A
    Report 71-16
Registrars of voters
    Election commissioners, appointment 51-16A
    Party representation 51-18, 19
    Registrars, appointment 51-15
Reports
    Audit of town accounts 44-39, 40
    Audit of trusts 41-53
    County commissioners 35-27
    County finances 35-28
    Investigation of accounts 44-46A
    Planning board 41-81C
    Regional school district 71-16
    State audit 44-39, 40
    Town accountant 41-58
    Town report 40-49
Representative town meeting
    Adoption of standard form 43A-1, 2
    Referendum on actions 43A-10
    Voting precincts 43A-3
Reserve fund, appropriations 40-6
Reserve fund, overlay 59-25
Retirement
    Acceptance of state law 32-28 (1), 28 (2) (a)
    Elected officers, notice of retirement 50-6A
    Retirement board, appointment 32-20 (4) (b)
    Small towns in county system 32-28 (3) (b)
    Veterans, incapacitated 32-56 to 60
Reward, offering for felony 276-10
Riots, dispersal by selectmen 269-1, 3
Road commissioner, temporary 41-40
Road commissioners, powers 41-63, 64

Rubbish disposal
  Approval of dumps 111-150A
  Contracts 40-4

S

Safety campaign, direction of selectmen 40-7A
School athletics, approval of travel expenses 71-47
School children, purchase of eyeglasses 40-5 (40)
School physician
  As health inspector 41-102A
  As town physician 41-106A
  As welfare agent 41-32A
Schools
  Borrowing for appropriation deficiency 71-34
  Deficiency in appropriation, order to provide 71-34
  Extended school services 71-26A, 26B, 26D
Sealer of weights and measures 98-34, 35
Selectmen
  Acting as other officers 41-21
    Board of health 41-21, 102
    Board of public welfare 41-31
    Board of survey 41-73
    Park commissioners 45-2, 5
    Planning board 41-81A, 81B, 81L
    Registrars of voters, in small towns 51-16
    Subdivision board of appeals, temporary 41-81Z
    Water commissioners 41-21, 69A
    Water commissioners, temporary 40-39A
    Zoning board of appeals, temporary 40A-14
  Appointment of certain officers 41-1, 21
  Bills and expenses of selectmen 41-56
  Control of town property 40-3
  Duties 41-20
  Election 41-1
  Estimates of expenses 41-59
  Executive secretary 41-23A
  Investigation of town departments 41-23B
  Oath of office 41-20
  Open meetings 39-23A, 23B, 23C
  Penalty for false election return 56-19
  Penalty for not electing 41-4
  Powers at state elections 54-18
  Powers under board of survey, not abridged 41-77
  Powers under planning laws, not abridged 41-81G
  Powers under subdivision laws, not abridged 41-81DD
  Repeal of authority for appointments 41-23
  Representatives of public safety commissioner 143-3A
  Special election for vacancy 41-10
  Term of office 41-1, 21
  Vacancies filled by selectmen 41-11, 22
  Vacancy in selectmen 39-11; 41-10
Settlement of town, determination of date 40-5 (27)
Sewage disposal works, land taking 83-6
Sewer commissioners
  Powers 41-65
  Selectmen as commissioners 41-21
Sewers
  Charges for use 83-16
  Laying out 83-1
  Regulations 83-10
  Special assessments 83-14, 15, 17, 19, 24
Shellfish constables, designation 130-98

Shellfish control and regulation 130-52 to 65
Shellfish purification plant 130-76 to 79
Shore (see Waters and shore)
Shore reservation
    Establishment 45-23A
    Indemnification of county 45-23C
Sidewalks
    Construction 83-25
    Special assessments, 83-26, 27
Sinking fund records, inspection 44-48
Slaughter houses 94-118 to 139, 111-151
Smoke regulation 140-133, 135
Snow removal
    Agreements with adjoining towns 84-5A
    Approval before appropriation 44-13
    Removal from private ways 40-6C
Sparrows and starlings, extermination 131-99
Special act, petition for revocation of acceptance 4-4A
Special assessments
    Betterments 80-1
    Sewers 83-14, 15, 17, 19, 24
    Sidewalks 83-26, 27
    Water pipes 40-42G, 42I
Steam engines for saw mills, regulation 140-115, 116, 119
Steam and hot water, laying of pipes 40-43
Street railways
    Bridges at crossing of railroad 161-131
    Construction, procedure 161-7
    Construction, taking of private land 161-58, 59
    Construction, use of private land 161-55
    Electric power lines (see Electric lines)
    Electricity, contract price 164-54
    Electricity, manufacture 161-45
    Electricity, purchase by town 164-52, 54
    Eminent domain 161-58, 59, 129
    Enforcement of laws, petition to court 161-142
    Extension of tracks 161-70
    Grade crossings, abolition 161-129
    Land taking, jurisdiction of selectmen 161-59
    Location, approval 161-7
    Location, change 161-7
    Location, petition 161-7
    Location, revocation 161-77
    Rate changes 161-112
    Regulation by selectmen 161-84, 85
    Repairs in highways 161-89
    Snow removal, regulations 161-85
    Tracks, discontinuance 161-86, 87
    Tracks, extension 161-70
    Tracks, relocation 161-71
    Tracks, removal 161-86
    Tracks, temporary location 161-72, 73
    Transportation area, establishment 161-143 to 146
    Transportation of baggage and freight 161-53
    Transportation of road materials 161-50
    Use of highways 161-7, 45
    Use of tracks, regulation 161-84, 85
    Warning of approach of cars 161-93
Strike or lockout, notice to state board 150-3
Subdivision board of appeals
    Appointment 41-81Z
    Selectmen as board 41-81Z
Subdivision control
    Board of appeals 41-81Z
    Public ways, powers of selectmen 41-81DD

Subdivision control law 41-81K et seq.
Suggestions, awards for employees 40-5 (43)
Sunday activities, licensing and regulation 136-2 et seq.
Sunday licenses (see Licenses)
Superintendent of insect pest control 132-13, 25
Superintendent of public works (see Board of public works)
Superintendent of sewer department 41-69
Superintendent of streets
    Appointment 41-21, 66
    Duties 41-68
    Service in two or more towns 41-67
    Service as water or sewer superintendent 41-69
Superintendent of water department 41-69
Survey board 41-73, 77
Surveyor's apparatus, standards 97-3
Swimming pools, control by selectmen 40-5 (25)

T

Tax anticipation notes 44-5
Tax assessors (see Assessor)
Tax collector (see Collector)
Tax reverted property, custodian 60-77B
Telegraph companies (see Telephone companies)
Telephone companies
    Action by selectmen, certification 166-22
    Complaint as to service or charges 159-24
    Construction of lines 166-21, 22
    Installations under highways 166-22A, 25
    Joint or identical locations 166-22
    Location of lines 166-21, 22
    Transfer of locations 166-22
    Use of highways 166-22, 25
    Violation of regulations 166-26
Telephone and telegraph lines
    Cutting of wires 166-39
    Regulation 166-25
    Regulation of private lines 166-23, 24
    Violation of regulations 166-26
Town clerk
    Absence of clerk 41-14
    Approval of bond 41-13
    Certificate of election 41-19A
    Removal in certain towns 41-19D
    Temporary clerk 41-14
    Term of office 41-1, 19B
    Vacancy 41-14
Town departments, investigation 41-23B
Town employees
    Half holiday, approval 41-110
    Hours of work 149-33A
    Indemnification 41-100A, 100B
    Insurance (see Insurance)
    Travel advances 44-66
    Travel expenses 40-5 (34)
    Veterans' employment 41-112
    Veterans' funerals, attendance 41-111C
Town meeting
    Absence of moderator 39-14
    Call for meeting 39-10
    Call other than by selectmen 39-10, 11
    Meeting in more than one place 39-10
    Refusal to call 39-12

Representative (see Representative town meeting)
Special meetings 39-9, 10
Subjects for meeting 39-10
Time of meeting 39-9
Warrant for meeting 39-10
Town officers
    Appointment by selectmen, in absence of other provisions 41-1
    Appointment by selectmen, by vote of town 41-21, 23
    Appointments to vacancies by selectmen 41-11
    Compensation 41-22
    Executive secretary to selectmen 41-23A
    Indemnification 41-100A
    Nomination by town caucus 53-121
    Open meetings 39-23A, 23B, 23C
    Payment and report of fees 40-21 (13)
    Retirement of elected officer 50-6A
    Selectmen acting as other officers 41-21
    Temporary finance officers 41-40
    Term of office 41-22
    Vacancies 41-11, 22
Town property (see Property)
Town report, annual 40-49
Trails and paths, town contribution for state construction 132-39
Transfer of appropriations 44-33B
Transportation area
    Board of trustees 161-146
    Establishment, for street railways 161-143 to 146
Treasurer
    Approval of bond 41-20, 35
    Assistant treasurer, approval 41-39A
    Borrowing, anticipation of reimbursements 44-6A
    Borrowing, before town meeting 44-5
    Employment of counsel 41-43A
    Indemnification 41-43A
    Library treasurer 78-10
    Removal 41-39B
    Temporary treasurer 41-40
    Vacancy 41-40
Tree warden
    Appointment 41-21, 106
    Duties 87-2, 4, 5
    Rules and regulations 87-2
    Temporary tree warden 41-40
Trust funds
    Audit and report 41-53
    Board of commissioners 41-45
    Selectmen as commissioners 41-45A

U

Urban redevelopment corporation, action of selectmen 121A-6, 13
Urban renewal plan, approval 121-26ZZ
Used car sales, regulation 140-57 to 66

V

Vehicles and carriages, regulation 40-22
Veterans' agent, appointment 115-3
Veterans, employment 41-112
Veterans' funerals 41-111C
Veterans, incapacitated, retirement 32-56 to 60
Veterans' services 115-10, 11, 12
Voting (see Elections)
Voting machines 54-34

W

War memorial trustees, temporary 41-105
Warrant for town meeting 39-10
Watchmen, requirement for hotels 143-46
Water, complaint as to furnishing by certain employers 149-106
Water and light commissioners, selectmen acting as such 41-21
Water and sewer board, selectmen acting as such 41-21
Water commissioners
    Powers and duties 41-69B
    Selectmen acting as such 41-21, 69A
    Selectmen acting temporarily 40-39A
Water meters, examination and testing 165-10
Water pipes
    Laying of water pipes 40-42; 82-25
    Laying of pipes other than by water company 165-8, 9
    Special assessments 40-42G, 42I
    Water pipes to another town 40-39
Water rates, petition for fixing rates in Hingham and Hull 92-16
Water supply
    Acquisition of water supply 40-39B
    Control of property 40-39E
    Control of system 41-69B
    Emergency water supply 40-40
    Eminent domain 40-39B
    Highway alterations 40-39C
    Pollution (see Pollution)
    Purchase of water rights 40-38
    Purchase of water sources 40-39B
Water and shore
    Alewives, regulation of fisheries 130-94; 158-15
    Beach district, establishment 40-12B
    Bridges over Charles River, consent to rebuilding 92-69
    Construction of wharf, sea wall or other structures 91-18
    Fence along canal or waterway, erection 88-12, 13
    Fish weirs, seines and traps, authorization 130-29
    Joint control of coastal fisheries 130-56
    Landing places or wharves, establishment and regulation 88-14
    Removal of stones, gravel sand or other protection against erosion 91-30A
    Shellfish constables 130-98
    Shellfish control and regulation 130-52 to 65
    Shellfish purification plant 130-76 to 79
    Shore reservation, establishment 45-23A, 23C
    Swamps (see Low lands and swamps)
Weighers of commodities and merchandise
    Measurers of lumber 96-7, 8
    Measurers of wood and bark 94-296, 297
    Weighers and measurers 41-85
    Weighers of beef 94-140
    Weighers of coal 94-238
    Weighers of fish 41-88, 89
    Weighers of grain 94-219, 221
    Weighers of hay 94-236
    Weighers of vessels 102-6
Weights and measures
    Enforcement of laws 98-32
    Sealer of weights and measures 98-34, 35
    Surveyor's apparatus, standards 97-3
    Water meters, testing 165-10
Welfare (see Public welfare)
Whistles and bells, regulation of use by employers 149-175
Wire inspection district 166-32
Wire inspector, appointment 166-32
Witnesses, summoning of 233-8

Z

Zoning
- Board of appeals, appointment 40A-14
- Boundaries of districts, public hearing 40A-6
- Building permit in violation 40A-12
- By-laws, adoption 40A-6
- By-laws, reconsideration 40A-8
- Enabling act 40A-1
- Exceptions, special permit 40A-4
- Hearing on adoption or change 40A-6
- Petition for variance or exception, reconsideration 40A-20
- Selectmen as temporary board of appeals 40A-14
- Zoning enabling act 40A-1 to 22

Date Due

Due	Returned	Due	Returned

Handbook for Massachusetts sel main
350.82M414p no.1 1960 C.2

3 1262 03292 9993

HSSL

350.82
M414p
no.1
1960
c.2

Printed in the USA
CPSIA information can be obtained
at www.ICGtesting.com
LVHW022311311023
762732LV00032B/795